Disclaimer

The information provided in this book is for general informational and educational purposes only and is not a substitute for professional advice. The author is not a licensed therapist, counsellor, or medical professional. The views expressed are the author's own and are based on personal experiences and research.

Readers should always seek the advice of a qualified professional for any health, financial, or legal concerns. The author and publisher assume no responsibility or liability for any damages or losses, whether direct or indirect, that arise from the use or misuse of the information contained in this book.

Medical Disclaimer

The content of this book is not intended to diagnose, treat, cure, or prevent any medical condition. The information shared is based on personal experience and should not be taken as medical advice. Always consult with a health care professional before making any changes to your health or wellness routines.

Names and Characters Disclaimer

Some names and identifying details have been changed to protect the privacy of individuals. Any resemblance to actual persons, living or dead, is purely coincidental.

CONTENTS

CHAPTER ONE

WELCOME TO THE POWER OF A PROMISE

CHANGE YOUR LIFE ONE PROMISE AT A TIME

Dear Reader,

Here we are—page one. You might wonder what you've gotten yourself into, and let me tell you, I get it. I know the feeling of searching for answers and encountering repetitive advice. But this book? This isn't about selling you a dream. It's about getting real about the promises we make and why they matter.

Because if life's taught me one thing, it's this: a promise to yourself is one of the most powerful things you can hold on to.

When I say promises, I'm talking about the commitments that get you through the hard days, not the big, flashy "New Year's resolution" kind. I'm talking about the small, meaningful ones that keep you going when everything feels like it's falling apart.

And trust me, I know what that feels like. I endured two divorces, lost everything, and rebuilt my life from the rubble. At one point, all I had left was a barn to call home, and even that felt like more than I deserved.

However, I didn't stay there. I found a way forward, not through luck or waiting for life to play nice, but by holding onto a promise: to myself, to my strength, and to the belief that I could rebuild. And here's the part that might surprise you: those promises saved me. They weren't grand or perfect, and sometimes they were downright laughable. But they were real. And I'm here to help you discover the same power in your own promises.

Life Doesn't Give Out Free Passes

Let's clear something up straight away. My story isn't here to win sympathy votes. I'm not sharing it because I think I've had it harder than anyone else. I'm sharing it because, no matter where you're at in life, the tough moments are the ones that teach you the most about yourself. They're what strip back the nonsense and shows you who you really are.

Now, I know if you've picked up any other self-help books, you've heard about "staying positive" or "manifesting your best self." Here's the truth they often leave out: all those ideas are just words until life backs you into a corner and forces you to figure things out.

> Reading motivational quotes is one thing, but facing life's challenges reveals your true strength.

And here's another reality check—life will keep testing you, no matter how much planning you've done. It'll throw you situations that you couldn't have predicted in a million years.

Plans? Life doesn't care about your plans. But a promise? Now that's different. A promise has weight. The one thing to hold on to when everything is uncertain.

Promises Are Your Anchor

The promises you make to yourself become your foundation. They're what keeps you grounded when everything else is up in the air. I'm not talking about some fluffy "wish upon a star" kind of thing. I'm talking about commitments you can count on when life feels like it's going sideways. And no, you don't have to get it perfect. None of us do. Even the most disciplined people slip up—yours included.

I remember times where I'd promised myself I'd "stick to the plan"—and life had other ideas. But every time I got back on track, every small promise I kept, it was like putting another brick in the wall. These small, simple promises keep you standing strong.

The Reality of Genuine Change

Listen, if you're hoping for a quick fix, this isn't it. Genuine change is messy. There will be days when even getting out of bed feels like an achievement. And when those days come, it's your promises that'll pull you through. They're the reminder that you're not giving up, not today.

Imagine this: life will have you believing it's all about the big, grand gestures. But let me save you some trouble. The truth is in the small things. Life isn't waiting for your masterpiece, it's watching you write your story, thought by thought. And that's what promises are—small thoughts, small actions that build your story, slowly but steadily.

Let me offer a bit of perspective here. Even the best of us don't receive training for every situation in life. Take the SAS—they're some of the best-trained forces in the world, but stick them in the middle of a family argument or a conversation with their teenage daughter about periods, and they're out of their depth like the rest of us.

> It's one thing to be prepared for a battle, quite another to navigate life's personal messes. No manual can prepare you for everything that is thrown at you in life, but promises? They are to keep you grounded and on the right path.

A Purpose to Get You Out of Bed

Now, let's talk about purpose. You don't need to have a perfect plan, but you need something that gets you up in the morning. Something you care about enough to keep going, even on the toughest of days. That's what promises are—they're what makes life feel real and worthwhile, even when the blows keep coming.

If you wake up every day with nothing to aim for, it's easy to feel you're just going through the motions. But a promise? It gives you a reason, a focus. It's something that would leave a gap if it were gone. And that's what we need—a commitment to something that pulls us forward, even on the days when it feels impossible.

Empathy and Perspective: Life Beyond Your Own Story

Let's get one thing straight—no one has the monopoly on struggle. We're all just trying to make it through. The next time you're tempted to judge someone else's journey, remember this: they're facing battles you might know nothing about. I've met people with almost nothing, yet they radiate a sense of joy and peace that most people only dream of. Why? Because they know happiness isn't about what you own but how you live.

Real Transformation: Keep it Real, Keep it Persistent

Here's the backbone of this book: integrity and kindness, especially to yourself. You're the person who knows yourself better than anyone, who's lived with yourself the longest. So why do we spend so much time convincing ourselves of things that are not true?

This journey isn't about being perfect or nailing every challenge. It's about facing what life throws at you, flaws and all, and choosing to keep going. **This is what the power of a promise is all about—getting back up, dusting yourself off, and having another go**. Because when you hold on to those promises, even the small ones, you're building a life that's rooted in something real.

As you read my story, I hope you see that experiences bring about resilience, strength, and determination.

The more you experience things in life, the more you will learn about yourself and who you truly are.

I hope you enjoy the journey. All my best wishes Scott

CHAPTER TWO

LET'S BEGIN

THE BOY WHO MADE A PROMISE

So here we go. Dive into these stories, pick up what resonates, and if the stories don't do it for you, skip to the practical bits at the end. Find what clicks and make it yours. And while you're at it, make a small promise—something just for you. Hold on to it. You will be amazed at how far one small promise can propel you.

Because actual change isn't about perfection. It's about showing up, making those promises, and keeping them, one step at a time. So let's get going. This is *The Power of a Promise,* and it all starts with you.

The world was a blur of laughter and wheels spinning. At ten, I buzzed with energy and believed promises were only for adults. They were about bills, keeping secrets, and things that didn't belong to the freedom of a summer's day. That afternoon—out on my bike with the lads, tearing around, showing off—everything changed.

"Dude, watch this!" Dave shouted, launching himself over a ramp. We cheered him on, each of us out to top the other's trick. My heart pounded with excitement. I was about to show them a jump they'd remember. This was going to be my moment—BMX legend in the making. But then, everything went dark. The laughter, the tricks, the sunny day—it all vanished.

"Scott! Wake up!" A woman's voice. A blur of faces. The dull hum of a machine. I opened my eyes to a room that felt sharp and bright. Sterile even. There was Mum's face, a tired smile that didn't reach her eyes. "You've been in an accident," she said, voice tight with worry.

"What happened?" My throat was sandpaper. I tried to remember, but my mind was blank, apart from shadows and figures. It felt wiped clean, like a chalkboard.

"A car hit you," she said, gently stroking my hair. "You're okay now, love."

The following days were a mess of faces, voices, and questions. Dad sat by my bed, looking worried, which wasn't like him. He was the stoic one, the one who barely batted an eyelid at anything. But now, he just sat there, face creased with worry. The doctors talked about a fractured skull, a broken nose, and stitches for my ear. They'd had to sew it back on, apparently, seven hours the operation took. The severity of it all didn't quite sink in.

Then, one day, a young officer came by for a chat. He looked like he was all business, but I saw a flicker of something in his eyes. "We spoke to the other boys, Scott. They say you were riding your bike, and then...you were errr hit by a car" and he quickly trailed off, his gaze drifting to some distant point.

"I remember riding... near the park," I said, feeling like I was searching for puzzle pieces in a mind that was blanker than an empty chalkboard. "There weren't any cars, I thought."

"That's what the boys said. A car hit you, but…" He didn't finish. It was like he couldn't bring himself to say anymore. I glanced at Dad, who looked down at the floor. Something wasn't right. I could feel it, the unspoken thing that sat heavy in the room.

After that, recovery was slow and painful. And with it came nightmares—dark, twisted dreams, the worse headaches you can imagine, and a mind filled with flashes of faces and feeling something cold gripping my throat. Every time I saw a group of lads on the street, my stomach would twist. I'd break out in a sweat, feeling hunted, feeling small.

"I can't go out there, Dad," I muttered one day, my voice barely more than a whisper. "They're waiting for me."

"They're not waiting for you, son," he said, though his face said something different. "You're safe now."

But it didn't convince me. I could feel that fear gnawing at me, an ever-present shadow. I became a different kid, always on guard, nervous, and never quite at ease.

Then came the day I was supposed to go to a football game I'd been excited about for weeks. As I neared the entrance, I saw a group of lads—same ones I could see in the shadows of my mind. They stood together in a huddle, laughing, with their faces half-hidden in the shadows. I froze. My legs felt like they'd turn and bolt at any second.

"No! Don't let them win," a voice boomed in my mind. It wasn't Mum's or Dad's, but something deeper, fiercer, like an echo of strength I didn't know I had. "You're strong. You're brave. Don't let fear control you."

I took a shaky breath, planted my feet, and walked toward them. My heart pounded like it was about to burst, but I kept going, step after step.

"It's him," one of them sneered as I got closer. "Too scared to walk past us?"

I didn't flinch. "I'm not scared of you," I said, voice steady, surprising even myself. "Not anymore."

They looked at each other, then back at me, a mix of surprise and disbelief on their faces. One of them laughed, sharp and harsh.

"Think you can blame us for what happened?" he said. "You think you could make us talk?"

I met his gaze, my fear replaced with something new—understanding. I realised they weren't the monsters I'd made them out to be. They were just kids, scared and unsure, like I'd been.

"I'm not saying anything," I said, a strength I'd never known filling me from somewhere deep. "But I'm not letting fear control me. You might've hurt me, but you won't break me."

And in that moment, something shifted. A warmth settled over me, an unbreakable resolve. I could feel it: I would not let this control my life. Not now, not ever.

"I promise," I said, my voice echoing with a certainty I hadn't felt before. "I promise I'll never be afraid like this again."

And I wasn't. The fear faded, replaced by a strength I never knew I had. I walked away from those boys without looking back, feeling lighter, feeling free.

From that day on, a promise wasn't just a word. It was a lifeline, a beacon, something I could hold on to when life got dark. A promise was my way of taking control, of saying to the world, "You can try to knock me down, but I'll keep standing."

That accident did more than leave scars and nightmares. It gave me the power to make promises that mattered. I learnt that a promise is more than an intention; it's a declaration, a commitment, a force that could see me through the worst of times. And that promise, the one I made as a scared ten-year-old, became my bedrock.

Through recovery, through the nightmares, through the fear of facing those lads again, that promise kept me going. I wasn't just a kid recovering from an accident—I was a boy transformed, determined to face life head-on.

So, if there's one thing to take from all this, it's this: promises are powerful. They're the commitments that keep you steady, the fire that pushes you forward. And when you find yourself standing in fear, facing a challenge that feels too big, remember that a promise—your promise—might just be the thing that saves you.

Chapter Three

MY PARENTS' DIVORCE

The Moment My Life Changed Forever

The news hit me like a punch in the face. I was twelve, snuggled under my duvet, half asleep, when Mum walked in. Her face was tight, like she was holding something in—something big. "I have something to tell you," she said, voice strained, as if each word was dragging something out of her. "And it can't wait."

And that was it. Mum said she and Dad were splitting up. Divorce. The word sat heavy, clinging to the air between us. My world—until that point solid, like a reliable, supportive and happy family—suddenly everything felt like it was crumbling from the inside out. How could this be happening without me even realising?

Then came the real spanner in the works: she'd be moving out. It was like the world had just collapsed around me. What about dad I said? I can't leave him on his own. I was supposed to be her priority. The one that mattered. But the world, apparently, had other plans.

Not long after, Mum moved out, taking my older brother with her. I stayed behind with Dad, holding on to what felt like the last remnants of our old life. But even that wasn't the same. Dad and I barely saw each other apart from eating our dinner on cardboard plates with plastic knives and forks (sounds bad, but we used to laugh about it). He'd leave early, throw a pound on the counter for lunch, and come home late, exhausted and tired. We'd pass each other like strangers the rest of the time.

School turned into enemy territory. Whispers followed me down the hallways, everyone's eyes on me like they knew something I didn't. In those days, it wasn't the done thing for parents to divorce. I was angry, hurt, and looking for someone—anyone—to blame. So I lashed out. I skipped classes, fell in with a rougher crowd, started fighting and started smoking pot, trading the classroom for the recce behind the school, and places I could disappear for a while without being found.

Then one night, Dad found me sprawled on the floor at home, a gash running down my back like that of a knife blade, from a fight I couldn't even remember. Blood everywhere. That should've been rock bottom, but it wasn't.

Then there was Tracy. My first love. We were chaos wrapped in teenage romance, two kids who thought we had all the answers. I got her name tattooed on my arm, thinking I looked tough—like a real rebel. But really, I was just a mess, hiding behind that tattoo and a relationship that, looking back, was my attempt to hold on to something, anything, that felt steady.

Dad caught me skipping school when I was sixteen. I hadn't been to a proper class in over a year and a half. The look on his face was one of disappointment mixed with something I couldn't quite name. But I was so far gone by then, I barely cared. School was a battlefield I wasn't ready to face.

Then came the blows I couldn't have seen coming. My grandma passed away, the light of our family gone just like that. Her smile, her warmth—things I thought would be around forever, turned to memories overnight. And not long after, we lost Grandad, too. Cancer. He left us like he'd lived—quietly. Dad took it hard, the grief heavy in the house like a fog. I wanted to help him, but I was drowning in my anger.

My aunt moved in around that time, trying to fill the silence with laughter and warmth. For a little while, it felt like the house had life in it again. But then Dad met someone new. A woman who would become my stepmum, bringing her son along too. They settled in, but that empty feeling inside me stayed put, like a hole I couldn't fill, no matter who else walked into our lives.

School became a distant memory, a place I no longer fitted into. My exams were a disaster. I needed a way out, something that would give me a clean slate. The army felt like my only option, a chance to reinvent myself.

Looking back, those years were a blur—a mix of loss, anger, and confusion that twisted me into someone I barely recognised. I was a kid, fumbling in the ruins of a life I no longer recognised, searching for a way out.

And if there's one thing I took from it all, it's this promises matter. I didn't know it at the time, but these early years were planting seeds—the idea that, even when everything else crumbles, a promise to yourself is what you can hold on to.

Chapter Four

SEEKING SOLACE IN THE ARMY

A Journey of Discipline and Self-Discovery

The day seared into my memory—4th of July, 1988. We hadn't even officially finished school, but I'd already checked out. I'd burned every bridge there, left behind nothing but a trail of trouble and a few bruised egos. School hadn't worked out, not for me, anyway. The only thing I carried forward was a promise I'd made to myself: I would not let fear run through my life.

The train ride was a blur—mostly tears and goodbyes. Tracy, my first love, was staying behind, and even though teenage love is about as steady as British weather, it still felt like leaving a piece of my heart. But as I looked out the window, I felt ready to take on something bigger, something that would shake up the chaos I'd left behind.

Stepping onto the army base felt surreal, like stepping into a movie. They wasted no time. They herded us straight into the barracks, gave us our kits, and lined us up for a haircut. I'd shaved my head beforehand, thinking I'd look the part, only to be told I'd missed a spot. The place was a sea of cocky sixteen-year-olds, each of us pretending we were tougher than we felt, trying to figure out who had "top dog" written on their forehead.

The days blurred into a relentless schedule: up at six, blankets folded like military art, breakfast wolfed down, then into hours of drills. And if anyone sneezed wrong, they would haul us out for another 10-mile run. I learned fast that in the army, mistakes were a team affair—you all paid the price, one blistered footstep at a time.

But nights they were worse. We'd hear whispers about "ghosts," the older recruits who'd sneak in, ready to dish out "lessons" to anyone who'd put a toe out of line. They called it "discipline," but to me, it felt more like hazing. Being told what to do was already pushing it for me—I wasn't exactly army material in the obedience department. I'd sneak out onto the balcony for a quick cig, just for a bit of control in a world that felt like a nasty prank gone wrong.

Then there were the "pranks" that went beyond reason. Like the times they emptied my locker through the window, or when they made me stand stark naked in the freezing cold while barking at me to "keep jogging."

Then came "murder ball." It was as brutal as it sounds: two teams, one massive ball, and the aim was to shove it across the other team's line. I was first to the ball, feeling invincible for about two seconds before ten lads from the other side crashed into me. My knees buckled, and I went down with a snap. They stretchered me off for X-rays and crutches, leaving me sidelined for weeks.

During that downtime, I accepted a pack of Rolos from another lad in the common room. Seemed harmless enough—until the next day, when the sergeant hauled me in front of him, accusing me of pinching rations.

"Course you did," they said. "Liverpool lad, can't keep his hands to himself." They didn't bother with my side of the story. Off I went to the Military Police Office for a night of "reflection"—or as they saw it, letting me stew while they played mind games.

After six weeks of this "education," I got some leave. Headed home to see Mum, who was looking worse for wear. Dad picked me up the next day, and we took a family holiday—a much-needed break from the madness. But even then, I found out I'd apparently "gotten engaged." Tracy had told everyone I'd proposed before leaving. Imagine my shock when Dad mentioned the engagement party plans. Nothing like a bit of news to keep you on your toes.

Back at the barracks, I had a chat with my stepdad, who told me Mum was in terrible shape. The divorce and my stint in the army had taken a toll on her. And that's when I knew the army wasn't where I needed to be. I'd learned enough, more than enough. It was time to move on, to come back to my family.

Looking back, the army was a crash course in lessons I wasn't expecting. It wasn't courage or discipline that stuck with me, but the realisation that sometimes the biggest battles aren't on the field—they're the ones you fight just to hold on to yourself.

Chapter Five

FACING THE CALL OF DUTY

Embracing Duty, Discipline, and Transformation Not

The Sergeant's office was thick with stale coffee and even staler authority. Across from me sat a man built like a tank, his face carved from years of barking orders and breaking wills. I shifted in my seat, trying not to let my nerves show.

"You signed a contract, soldier," he rumbled, like he'd rehearsed it a thousand times. "The army needs you."

I took a breath, determined to hold my ground. "I am tired of being here, Sergeant." I want out." The words landed solid, even though my stomach was in knots.

"Then you'll need your parent's signature on the release forms," he said, each word clipped and cold. They sent me back to my dorm, saying, "Alright, we'll phone your dad and see what he says." I waited, pacing, running my hand along the edge of the bunk, feeling that itch to just get out, to break free from this place that felt less like an institution for building men and more like a prison yard.

A bit later, they called me back in, faces blank and clipped as they told me, "He thinks it would be good for you to stay, says you need the discipline—that it'll make you into a man."

And there it was—the dead end I half-expected. My dad, my legal guardian, was absolutely against me leaving, convinced the army was exactly what I needed to straighten out, learn responsibility, become that "real man" he always talked about. (I found out 30 years later that this wasn't even true, a prank who knows, but a costly one at that)

But for me, every day felt like pushing a boulder up a hill. Their idea of discipline was crushing my spirit, a constant clash between who I wanted to be and the version of me they were so determined to shape. They saw an institution to sharpen me, to build me up; I saw a cell, somewhere that wasn't made for the person I was or the life I wanted.

Every day became a tug-of-war. Not just with my squad and the officers, but with myself—between my desire to escape and the weight of their expectations dragging me back.

The thought of waiting—trapped in this endless military limbo—was enough to make me feel like I was suffocating. My mind raced, searching for a way out, and then it hit me: Mum. If anyone could cut through the nonsense, it was her. She'd never been one for red tape, and she knew how to get things done.

I found the payphone in the hallway and dialled her number. The phone buzzed, and then her familiar voice answered, calm but firm.

"Tell him I want to speak to his commanding officer," she said, her voice carrying that no-nonsense edge I loved. "And if that doesn't work, tell him I'll be ringing the local news."

I almost laughed at the thought, but her words gave me a boost of confidence as I walked back into the Sergeant's office, standing taller.

"Sergeant, my mum would like to speak to your commanding officer," I said, feeling a surge of defiance.

He snorted. "That's not how this works, soldier."

"Well," I replied, "then she'll be calling the local news. Pass that along to your commanding officer."

His face went red, a vein pulsing at his temple. "You can't just do that!" he shouted, slamming his fist on the desk.

But I didn't flinch. I'd had enough of being treated like some cog in their machine. He glared, but after a long, tense silence, he finally relented. "Fine," he muttered, barely keeping his temper. "I'll get your mum on the line with my commanding officer."

As I waited, relief sank in. Mum was fighting for me when I'd nearly given up fighting for myself. It was a glimmer of hope I hadn't felt in ages.

That night, I packed my things, finally feeling the weight of the decision. Leaving the army wasn't a small thing. It wasn't a decision I made lightly, but it was mine. And that made all the difference.

Packing was a mission in itself. I shoved my life into a flimsy suitcase, barely able to zip it shut. Then Mum called again. "Just a few more days, love," she said, but I could hear the strain in her voice. I knew "a few more days" was more hopeful than factual—they'd keep me here as long as they could. Another cog in the system.

Back at the Military Policeman's office for another "re-evaluation," they steered me into a cold room with walls that felt like they were closing in on me. Sergeant Miller, a man built like a brick wall and with the personality to match, glowered from behind his desk. "You think you can just walk away? This is a commitment, boy! You made your choice. Now live with it!"

His words were like ice water on frayed nerves. All I wanted to do was shout, "You do not know what this is like for me!" But before I could, another MP—Sergeant Jones, who was younger and had a sneer that made you want to smack it right off his face—leaned in, voice dripping with disdain.

"You're just scared," he said, all too pleased with himself. "Think you're too good for this? You're just a scared kid."

I clenched my jaw, refusing to let them see the frustration simmering under the surface. I'd made a promise to myself long before this: I would let no one control me with fear again. I wasn't feeling scared. I was just a kid trapped in a system that wanted to grind me down.

"Knobheads," I muttered, loud enough for them to catch.

For the next three days, they tried to break me. They shoved, they yelled, they tried every trick in their book. I stood my ground, fighting back in my way, refusing to let them win. Every day felt like a slow battle of wills, a game of endurance I couldn't afford to lose.

"Why are you so stubborn?" Jones asked, his voice dripping with irritation.

I met his gaze, steady as I could. "Because," I said, "this is all bollocks, and I'm stronger than you think."

In that moment, it felt like a victory—a small one, maybe, but a victory all the same. I was still trapped, but I refused to let myself be beaten. Not by a long shot. And as that tiny flame of defiance burned inside me, I knew this was just the beginning. Soon, I'd be walking out of this place, ready to start a life of my making.

CHAPTER SIX

BREAKING FREE

MOVING FORWARD

The day I walked out of those army gates, I felt like I'd shed a skin I'd outgrown. A mix of relief and just a hint of fear hit me. After all, they had trained me to follow orders, but the Army? It had felt like trying to shove a square peg (me) into a round hole. My mates had thrived in that rigid structure. Me? I craved freedom, a sense of purpose that didn't involve saluting at dawn.

I wasn't exactly sure what this new life was going to look like, but I was determined to find out. Gloucestershire became my fresh territory—a place where I could hit "reset" on life. But moving somewhere with no friends, no job, and no idea of what was next felt a bit like standing on the edge of a cliff, hoping there'd be something soft to land on. Still, I wasn't keen on going back to my dad, who'd wanted me to stay in the Army anyway (had I of known the truth, I maybe would have gone back there). My stepdad, though, had a different take. He believed in education and saw potential beyond me being "Army lad." He even bought me a motorbike to get around, which felt like my first real taste of freedom.

To keep my new life afloat, I started taking on odd jobs here and there. It was the first time I'd been driven by something inside me—a promise I'd made to myself to make something out of this fresh start, even if I wasn't sure what "something" was yet.

Then there was Tracy, the girl whose name I'd recklessly tattooed onto my arm back when I thought young love was the be-all and end-all. She came to stay with me, but everything felt... off. The spark we'd had flickered like a dying match. Maybe it was because I'd turned down her plans for an engagement, or maybe it was just that, at sixteen, I couldn't see myself tied down. I wanted to break free, not swap one cage for another.

Then, one day, my mate Mark came over. He was about to join the Army himself and wanted the inside scoop. I tried to keep things light—the camaraderie, the sports. I wasn't about to be the guy who dashed his dreams before he even got started.

We ended up talking about Tracy. I sensed he was holding something back. After a bit of probing, he finally cracked. "Mate, I saw her. Tracy... she was with one of your army mates. They were kissing."

It felt like a punch in the face. The betrayal hit hard. All those nights away, all the sacrifices, and for what? I grabbed my phone, hands shaking, and dialled her number.

"That's it," I said, barely containing my anger. "We're done. Never call me again." And just like that, I hung up, cutting her out of my life with one sharp word. The pain was raw, but alongside it, I felt a strange sort of release. I didn't need anyone who couldn't see my worth. I'd fought to stand on my own two feet before, and I wasn't about to let one heartbreak set me back.

As the weight of that last goodbye sank in, I looked down at my arm, at the now-ironic tattoo of her name. I'd been young and stupid, thinking love at fourteen could be forever. Now it was just ink on skin, a reminder of a chapter I was ready to close. Getting rid of it would be a battle for another day.

This was the beginning of a new chapter, a clean slate that was entirely mine.

CHAPTER SEVEN

FREEDOM ON TWO WHEELS

BACK TO COLLEGE WE GO

The roar of my motorbike was like a war cry, breaking the silence of the countryside when I pulled up in the car park at college for the first time. Sixteen and a half, a GCSE dropout with barely a plan to my name, and here I was, back in college, taking a crack at something new. I could feel the thrill of possibility mixed with the taste of freedom, like standing on a cliff edge, ready to dive.

"Oi, you're the new lad, yeah?" A bloke leaned over, all friendly with a curious grin. "Name's Liam. What's yours?"

"Scott," I answered, grinning back. I felt surprised by how natural it was. College was miles away from the Army life—no barking sergeants, no unyielding routine. Here, people actually smiled when they said hello. But with all that freedom, I started feeling a bit... lost.

Structure, that's what I was used to. The Army had been all about constant motion—physically, mentally. But here, in a classroom, I felt like a boat adrift. Every dull lecture only made the "what ifs" louder in my head. I didn't know where I was going, but it was clear I needed something more than this.

"You heading down the pub with us tonight?" Liam's arm landed on my shoulder, all casual.

"Yeah, alright," I replied automatically. Didn't take much convincing—I wasn't turning down a pint. But saying yes felt a bit like following the tide, not really steering the ship.

Days melted into weeks, then months. I found comfort in the gym, footy, and mates like Liam. We bonded over shared laughs and countless rounds at the pub. But the spark? It was missing. College life felt like the Army without the purpose. Like I was a cog in a machine that made little sense.

One day, Mr Davies, the head of the year, summoned me for "a chat."

"Scott," he started, eyebrows raised in that classic look of disappointment, "we need to talk about your progress."

The lectures I'd missed, the assignments I'd ignored—it all caught up with me. His face illustrated the gravity of my lack of interest.

"You're not keeping up with your work," he said, his voice firm but not unkind. "We are going to have to ask you to leave."

I nodded, feeling like someone had let the air out of my tyres. "I understand," I mumbled. I had been expecting this conversation. Somehow, hearing it out loud just made it sting that much more.

When I told my mum and Chris, it didn't go down well. "What are you doing, Scott?" Mum's voice was tight with worry, a hint of anger. "You had a fresh start—this was supposed to be your future!"

And I got it, I really did. I didn't want to mess things up, but none of it felt right. I looked back at her, trying to find the words. "Mum, I don't know what I'm thinking," I said, feeling as lost as ever. "I'm just... I'm not happy there."

Chris, my stepdad, wasn't one to mince words. "And what now, Scott? What's your big plan?" His voice had that edge of concern laced with frustration.

Truth was, I didn't have a plan. I felt like I was swimming in a sea of non options, with no land in sight.

"Chris, I need time to figure it out," I said, feeling the weight of my own words. "I'll find a job, something that feels like me." I had to admit, for once, I was envious of people who had everything mapped out.

That night, lying in bed, the quiet felt heavier than usual. I stared at the ceiling, asking myself, "Who do I even want to be? What would actually make me happy?"

Those questions felt like they'd been haunting me for ages, but now, there was no avoiding them. It was time to answer them, or at least take a good shot at them.

"I'll find a job I can actually enjoy," I whispered to myself, feeling a strange sense of calm. "I'll make a life I want to live." Then turning it into a promise and saying it aloud gave it weight.

It was just a simple promise to myself, but it felt like the beginning of something real, something I could hold on to. I set off, no longer just reacting to life, but choosing my path forward.

CHAPTER EIGHT

SELLING DREAMS

REBUILDING FROM RUINS

Sitting in the front room of my mum's house, I felt like I was back in a cage I'd only just broken out of. The familiar walls seemed to close in the room, holding the ghosts of a dozen failed plans. But as I flipped through the newspaper, past the ads for groceries and dodgy used cars, a job listing stood out: Junior Estate Agent—Training Provided. It was like a lighthouse in a sea of doubt.

"This is it," I announced, as if the words alone could make it true. Mum and Chris looked up, a bit surprised, as I told them about the job.

"An estate agent, eh?" Chris gave a half-smile. "Let's see how you get on, Scott." Something in his tone made me feel apprehensive. Was I good enough for the job? What if I didn't get it? What then?. With his help, we polished my CV, and I poured everything I had into the cover letter. This wasn't just an application—it was my ticket to something real.

A few nail-biting days later, my phone buzzed. "It's them!" I said, barely able to believe it. I picked up, palms sweaty, as they offered me an interview. "Next week," they said. I could hardly keep still, practically bouncing around the room.

Mum was on board straight away. "We'll get you a proper suit," she said, giving me that mum-look, one part pride and one part "you'd better not muck this up." In the shop window, I saw myself—a lad in a suit, slightly oversized, but somehow it made me look... ready. For the first time, I saw a glimpse of who I could be.

The day of the interview, I walked in, nerves humming like an electric current. The office was all glass and polished desks, the interviewers serious and suited. They started with the usual questions, but then came the test—a Sellotape dispenser plonked on the desk.

"Sell this to us," one of them said, deadpan.

For a split second, my mind went blank. Sellotape? But I remembered my promise—to push through. I took a deep breath and let the words flow, asking questions, listing features, even throwing in, "Would you like it gift-wrapped?" I was rambling, but there was something liberating in it—a sense that, for once, I could just be myself.

To my shock, they laughed. "You're hired!" one of them said, and I walked out of there on top of the world. I made myself a promise: "I'll be the best estate agent they've ever seen."

Not long after, I passed my driving test, and my boss handed me the keys to a company car. "Take it for a spin to Liverpool," he said. "Show your brother what you've achieved." The drive felt surreal—me, in my car, headed up north to show off my success. I'd made it in my way.

In Liverpool, I met Mark, a mortgage broker full of energy and ambition. He talked about Brian Tracy, visualising success, making big moves. "Don't waste a minute of your time," he'd say, slapping me on the back. "You're meant for more than this." For the first time, I believed I could have it all.

Life moved in fast-forward. Open houses, contracts, and late-night pints with Mark became my new rhythm. "You're a star, Scott," he'd tell me, like it was already a fact. I felt unstoppable, a kid turned professional, navigating a world I'd only ever dreamed of.

Then, like a wave I never saw coming, the housing market crashed. Everything I'd built, every late night, every sale, crumbled like a sandcastle washed away by the tide. My branch closed, my flat was gone, and the car was no longer mine. Just like that, my dreams turned to dust.

I found myself back in the front room, staring at the faded wallpaper, a hollow ache where my hope used to be. It was as if all those promises I'd made, to myself, to my family, were just whispers in a storm. My stepdad, seeing me in that state, sat down next to me.

"It's not the end, Scott," he whispered. "This is just a setback. We all get them."

As I stared at the walls, the ones I'd always seen as a trap, I felt something shift. The words he'd said flickered inside me, like the embers of a fire that refused to die. I could feel the familiar frustration turning into something else—determination. A voice in my head, quiet but growing stronger, reminded me of that first promise I'd made to myself: I won't let this beat me.

Taking a deep breath, I made another promise, right there in that room. "I'll rebuild," I whispered to myself. "This isn't the end; it's just the start of something new."

And as I said it, I knew that no matter how many times I had to start over, I'd keep going. Because this time, I wasn't just selling dreams. I was building them—one promise at a time.

Chapter Nine

STARTING OVER IN SHROPSHIRE

Promises, Parties, and a New Path

Chris sat me down, his expression serious, like he was about to hand me a life sentence. "Look, Scott, I'm sorry about this, but we're going to have to move. I've got a new job in Shropshire, and you're coming with us." Another move. I could feel the weight settle on my shoulders—a familiar, sinking sensation. A whole new town, unfamiliar faces, and unknown places to fit into. I'd have to start over again, while the friends I'd just made would fade into memories.

But there it was again, that promise I'd made to myself, the one about living a life without fear. No matter how daunting or unknown, I'd vowed not to let fear call the shots. So, swallowing my nerves, I treated this as an opportunity. Maybe Shropshire was the blank slate I needed.

When we arrived, I didn't have a clue what I was going to do next. The place felt like the middle of nowhere, but I thought, "Why not give college another shot?" Sure, it was a gamble, but I figured I'd somehow blag my way through it, like I always did. At least it would keep me busy and, hopefully, keep me out of trouble.

College was a breath of fresh air, or at least I tried to convince myself it was. There was a certain buzz in being the "new guy," and I quickly found myself surrounded by a cast of characters who kept things interesting. Jason was the joker, always ready with some off-the-wall comment, and then there was Cosy, a giant of a lad with a heart as soft as marshmallow. We spent hours in the common room, slinging stories back and forth, fuelled by cheap vending machine coffee. I only found out later that Cosy, also known as "General Cosy," was practically considered royalty in one of the town's football gangs, the EBF.

Days at college blended into nights out on the town, a blur of pounding bass, flashing lights, and the haze of late-night raves. It felt like a release valve, a chance to forget everything that felt broken and just live in the moment. And right there, in the middle of it all, I met Sarah. She was a live wire, with this spark that lit up every room she walked into. We were chaos together—drawn to each other like moths to a flame.

But the rumours started before long. People began whispering that I was dealing heroin. Me? I'd never touched the stuff, but all it took was my Scouse accent and a bit of a mystery for suspicion to stick. The town didn't take kindly to "outsiders," and soon the whispers followed me like shadows. I tried to brush it off, but the weight of it all started pressing down, slowly but surely.

What had been my escape—college, parties, the laughter with new mates—felt like a prison. I was drifting further and further away from any sense of purpose. Eventually, I just... stopped going. Dropped out with little ceremony, feeling like I'd failed yet again.

Back at my mum's house, I felt the familiar frustration clawing at me. But then, in a moment of clarity, I thought back to my old job as an estate agent. I remembered the thrill of closing a sale, of feeling like I was good at something, like I could actually make a mark. It sparked something, a flicker of determination. I wasn't done yet.

I scanned the job ads, and two stood out: a Junior Manager position at an insurance broker, and an entry-level spot at an estate agency. I polished up my CV, put on a suit, and walked into both interviews feeling like I had something to prove. Maybe even to myself. After weighing it up, I took the insurance job. There was something in the challenge of managing a team, the promise of a structured path, that felt like the right fit.

The work was no joke—long hours, relentless demands, and a steep learning curve. But I threw myself into it, determined to make something of myself. Within a year, I'd climbed to Branch Manager, handed over my set of keys and a shiny company car. For the second time, it felt like the world was opening up.

However, I still spent weekends back in Liverpool, and it felt like stepping into a different life. A whirlwind of late nights, wild parties, and that reckless abandon I thought I'd left behind. It was addictive—the freedom, the thrill. But deep down, I could feel the cracks forming. It was as if I'd built this life on shifting sand, a structure that couldn't hold.

Looking back, I can see it was the calm before the storm. The success, the freedom, the wild weekends—they were thrilling, sure. But I knew a wake-up call was on its way, one that would hit harder than any before. The real question was whether I'd be ready for it.

Chapter Ten

DUST, DIGNITY

The Day I Walked Out

Running my branch felt like I was on Top of the World again. Merryll, my assistant, was steady as a rock, the sort who could practically run the place herself. Then there was Linda, our very own anti-saleswoman, who wouldn't sell a thing on religious grounds. God only knows who thought a sales role was her calling. But there she was, ever-cheerful and utterly resistant to, you know, actually doing the job.

The drive to work each morning was a thrill in itself. I'd just picked up a Vauxhall Nova Sport, and it handled like a dream around those winding corners. The office was pristine, the clients polite, and I was thriving on hitting those targets. I felt like I was building something, setting my little empire in motion.

Then came Christmas. After a year of grinding, I'd decided a break was in order. I booked a trip to the Dominican Republic, left a temp manager to hold the fort, and off I went, suitcase in one hand and a cocktail in the other. When I got back, though, something was off. An email sat there in my inbox, summoning me to a managers' meeting—urgent. I felt that familiar tightness in my chest; the sort that tells you someone's about to drop a bomb.

Turns out, I wasn't wrong. The General Manager was on a warpath. He was fuming over missed report deadlines, and then my name came up. Turns out my temp hadn't filed a single report over the holidays. Without skipping a beat, the GM declared he'd be docking forty percent of my wages.

"Hang on a minute," I thought, feeling my blood rise. "It's Christmas, for crying out loud! And you think I'm gonna take this on the chin?" That night, I sat down and wrote a letter. Not a polite one, mind. It was scathing, every line dripping with the promise I'd made to myself years ago—not to let anyone treat me like a doormat. I laid out every legal reason they couldn't just hack my wages like that and finished with a line about "legal recourse" if they tried it again.

The next morning, the phone rang. It was the GM, sounding like he was about to pop a vein. "How dare you send that letter?!" he barked. "Pack up. You're done here!"

But I didn't flinch. I knew he was bluffing—he had to be. Sure enough, an hour later, HR called, all apologetic. "It seems there's been a mistake," they muttered. "You're reinstated. Back to work tomorrow." Clearly, they'd realised sacking me for defending myself might not look so hot in court.

I figured the worst was over. But then, the next day, the Area Manager showed up. He slid a written warning across the desk. "You left... dust... on the photocopier." Deadpan. He even kept a straight face.

I looked him right in the eye. "Dust. On the photocopier. Are we serious here?"

"Company policy," he replied, still stone-faced. I could see the game they were playing now. Every little thing was a pretext to undermine me, to make me toe the line. It was small-time bullying, dressed up in corporate nonsense.

The pressure built week by week. They'd criticise every detail, invent reasons to "have a word," like some twisted office bootcamp. It was laughable, really. They thought they could grind me down, but they didn't know that I'd made a promise to myself—one that wasn't about to be broken.

One day, after yet another absurd "chat" about the coffee machine being "out of alignment," I'd had enough. I knew I deserved better than this petty power play. So, I packed my things, took one last look at the office I'd built, and walked out without a second thought.

That was it—a last promise to me. No more bullying, no more bending. Whatever came next it would be on my terms. I'd find something better, something where I didn't have to fight for basic respect. I walked out that door, leaving dust and nonsense behind, and never looked back.

CHAPTER ELEVEN

THE ALMOST-PROMOTION

THE DEFINITELY-NOT REDUNDANCY

The insurance job was just a warm-up—a way to hone my skills for the real thing, the big leagues. I'd been itching for something with more substance, and that's when I saw it: a training company, looking for someone to sell software to insurance brokers. It had my name written all over it, or at least it felt that way. I fired off my CV and a cover letter that could've convinced the Queen herself to give me a shot. Then came the wait.

A few days later, my phone buzzed. They wanted an interview. Perfect. I was ready for this, though as I sat in their car park on the day, my hands were shakier than I'd expected. This wasn't just another job. At 21, I'd already tasted disappointment, and I wasn't eager for a second helping. But this... this felt like it could actually go somewhere.

The interview was a proper test of nerves. First, they had me do a psychological assessment that was so intense; I left wondering if they'd diagnose me on the spot. Then came a two-hour grilling and, as the cherry on top, a presentation. They said I could pick any topic, so I went with what I knew best—myself. I spun a tale of grit, passion, and drive, painting a picture of a guy they had to hire.

When I walked out, I felt exhausted but quietly confident. A week later, they called back: round two, just me and one other candidate, final show-down style. I gave it everything. I made sure every answer, every handshake, and even the pitch of my voice screamed, "hire me." The pay was better, the car was new, and the potential was... well, it felt limitless.

Sure, it meant moving a hundred miles away, but that didn't matter. Sarah, my girlfriend from college, was off to university up the road. I had it all mapped out: a few months of commuting, then we'd have our own place, our own life. Everything was falling into place.

The job was everything I'd hoped for and more. I was on the road, travelling around the UK, meeting new people, making deals. I was living the dream, or at least a version of it. Weekdays were for work; weekends were for Liverpool, football, and late nights. My life felt unstoppable, like I'd cracked the code of success.

Then, one Friday afternoon, I got the call.

"Scott, it's Sam," my manager's voice came over the line. She sounded serious, but there was an edge of excitement. "Can you come in tomorrow? The bosses want to talk to you. It's about a promotion."

A promotion. I nearly dropped the phone. This was it. I'd only been there a year, and I was already getting a nod from the top. That night, I could barely sleep, visions of a bigger office, a fancy title, and a pay rise spinning around my head.

The next morning, I waltzed into the office with a grin that could've lit up the building. But instead of a warm welcome, the security guard met me, looking like he'd rather be anywhere but here.

"Scott, can you come with me, please?" he said, and something about his tone made my heart skip. He led me up to the General Manager's office, and that's when I saw it: the dreaded envelope. Without so much as a "how do you do," the GM slid it across the desk.

I tore it open, reading the words that still sting to this day. Redundant. With immediate effect. My world crumbled right there in that sterile office. I'd given everything to this job, thrown myself into it—and now, without so much as a "thanks for your efforts," they were tossing me aside.

It got worse. They took my fuel card, leaving me with no fuel in the car as I hadn't filled up because I was so excited to get there. I felt my face burning with humiliation as they escorted me out of the building. I was furious, heartbroken, and, more than anything, blindsided.

I drove home in a daze. Sarah, our flat, my future—all of it had vanished in the time it had taken me to open a letter. I got home and sat there, staring at the wall, feeling like life had cheated me. I'd worked so hard, pushed myself so far, and yet here I was, back to square one.

For a few days, I let the anger fester, wallowing in self-pity and frustration. But then, slowly, a new determination took root. This was not the end of my journey. This would not be the end of my story, either. I'd get to Reading, I'd be with Sarah, and I'd build something even better.

I just didn't know how yet—but I knew I'd find a way.

Chapter Twelve

THE ROAD TO NOWHERE

Car Covered In Pidgeon Poo

The drive home was a foggy blur of rage and disbelief. Every mile felt like I was drifting further from my future and closer to a dead end. I'd left that office with nothing but a bruised ego and a few paltry months of severance—the type of insult that makes your blood boil. I gripped the wheel, my knuckles going white, and for a moment, I wondered if I was even seeing the road or just feeling it as the world spun around me.

Pulling into the driveway, I parked under the old oak tree out front. It felt silly, but I wanted some cover, some shield from the day's cruelty. I left the car there for weeks—let it gather dust, leaves, and pidgeon poo. When they came to take it back, they found it anything but pristine. I couldn't help but let a bitter laugh slip out. Petty? Maybe. But after the punch in the face I'd just taken, it felt like a fitting send-off.

Later that night, Sarah came over with a bottle of Baileys. Bless her. We sat on the porch steps, the night air thick with our unspoken fears. I knew what was on her mind. With no steady job, no income, and no chance of getting a place down south near her, our plans seemed as unreachable as ever.

"So, what's next?" she asked gently, her fingers tracing the outline of the bottle cap.

I took a deep breath, trying to swallow the knot in my throat. "I think... I think I'm going back to college," I said, barely recognising my voice. Another college attempt. It felt like reaching out for an old, worn lifeline. But maybe this time would be different. I'd be a mature student in environmental science, aiming to get through the foundation year and on to a degree.

Sarah looked at me, her eyes steady. "You'll do it," she said, and somehow, I believed her. The promise I'd made to live without fear came roaring back, reminding me I'd been through worse, and I wasn't about to let some corporate tossers be the end of my dreams.

We sat there, looking out into the dark, each of us holding onto the hope of a future we were determined to make real.

The next few months were a blur of study and late shifts in a metal pressing factory. I spent every weekend I could with Sarah, saving up and stretching out my pay to afford the petrol and the promise of a better life. Every penny I made felt like another brick in the foundation of that life we were building together.

As exams loomed, so did the anxiety. I was rubbish at exams—a fact I'd made peace with ages ago—but I couldn't fail. This time, there was too much on the line. I was doing this for us, for the future we deserved.

Then the results came in: I'd passed. Not just passed—I'd exceeded my own expectations. I'd earned a place at Reading University. Sarah couldn't stop grinning, and for the first time, neither could I.

The summer flew by as we prepped for the move. I secured a room with Sarah and her friends, a new home filled with excitement and the thrill of something real. Standing there, knowing I'd made it, I finally felt like all the struggles, all the nights spent doubting and working and scraping by, had led me here.

I wasn't just another young guy drifting from job to job, trying to figure things out. I was Scott, the man who'd dared to hope when hope seemed impossible. And I wasn't alone in it. We were finally on our way. The road ahead might have looked uncertain, but for the first time, I was driving towards a future I could believe in.

CHAPTER THIRTEEN

THE DJ DREAM

THE HARD CHOICES

When it was time to head down to Reading, my stepdad gave me a lift. I had enough gear with me to start a small business, including my beloved decks. I had already stuffed the room with the soundproofing materials I had ordered in advance. I needed a proper setup so I could DJ without rattling every window in the neighbourhood. I didn't just like DJing; it was my entire focus. The new start, the studying—all of it was secondary to the music.

My first lecture passed in a haze. Surrounded by younger faces fresh out of halls, I sat there as they formed their little packs. I could feel the social circles closing up around me, but that was alright. I hadn't come to Reading to make mates—I was here to make music.

It didn't take long to track down the guy in charge of DJ bookings at the university. I went straight to him, laid it all out. After some back-and-forth, he agreed to give me a trial night at the student union. I prepped like a madman, scoping out what might get the crowd bouncing, and on the night, the place was on fire. Students loved it, and so did the booking manager. He started offering me regular gigs at bars around town—the Newt and Cucumber, a wine bar I can't remember, and the odd guest night at the local club. But when they suggested I play for free "for the experience," I had to laugh. Experience? I needed to eat.

Before long, I was DJing most nights, taking on weddings and parties to cover my rent. It wasn't the party scene I'd imagined; half the time, I was flying solo. But the crowd's energy, the thrill of it all, kept me going. Uni, though? Boring as hell. I'd rock up, half-interested, and by the time the lecture wrapped, I'd be counting down to my next gig.

Sarah, meanwhile, had got a job at our favourite local pub. She fit in nicely, partly thanks to me already knowing half the people there. But my social life had its own quirks. One night, some bloke at the bar started throwing weird comments my way. After he wouldn't shut up, I took him aside and said, "Mate, keep it up, and I'll have to give you a slap." To my surprise, he apologised and said he thought he was just being funny. Turns out, he was one of the richest guys I'd ever met—him and his mates owned a computer company.

In time, he offered me a part-time gig at the company to help cover my costs. It was a decent setup: a few afternoons and Saturdays, with DJing on top. Eventually, though, it was too much to juggle. The computer gig started feeling like a proper job, with more structure, stability. I knew I had to choose, and I leaned into the "sensible" option. I didn't fully grasp how far DJing might've taken me back then. Looking back, it's a regret, but I thought I'd made the grown-up decision.

Chapter Fourteen

LEAVING UNIVERSITY

Finding Family

The lecture hall was stifling, thick with that judgemental silence only academics can muster. I'd made my decision: I was walking out, abandoning my Environmental Biology degree, and the lecturer made sure I knew the consequences. "You won't be able to come back," he warned, with that slight curl of disdain in his voice, as if my choice was an affront to the very institution. But I'd already weighed my options. A degree felt like a pretty piece of paper, but the real world? That was a different beast altogether, and I was already carving out my space in it.

I didn't vanish into obscurity, though. Instead, I found my spot in the community, down at The College Arms, where the regulars knew my face better than the students knew my name. It was different, unplanned, and somehow felt like I was building something real.

One night, I noticed a group of Asian guys I'd once chatted with hanging around outside the pub. Standing close together, they seemed as if they were exiled. "Why are you guys out here?" I asked, glancing at the warm lights inside.

"Not allowed in, mate,". One of them shrugged, suggesting a subtle exclusion, as if they had drawn an invisible line on the floor. I could feel that old promise rising in me—the one about facing down fear and pushing back against prejudice. Without a second thought, I grabbed a seat outside and joined them, and soon we were chatting like old mates.

Over time, the frostiness thawed. It wasn't long before I suggested they come inside. "Look, the landlord's a decent guy. He's not the kind to get caught up in this nonsense," I said. And I was right. Tom, the pub landlord—gruff as sandpaper but with a heart buried somewhere in there—welcomed them with a grin and a pint.

That little gesture changed everything. The College Arms became our haven, a place where friendships blossomed in the glow of pints and shared laughs. We were an unlikely crew: pub regulars, students, and those of us who never quite fit in anywhere else. It was like we'd built our own little world within the pub walls, a misfit family bound together by laughter, shared stories, and support.

Then Ranj, one of my mates from the group, started dating Tom's daughter, Claire. They were a perfect match, their love cutting through cultural boundaries without a second thought. Their son, little Tom, was born soon after—a tiny bridge uniting two worlds. And there he was, a living testament to what could happen when we ignored the old divisions.

But life's never content to just let things be. News hit us like a punch to the face—Tom, the heart and soul of The College Arms, had cancer. He battled it with everything he had, but in the end, it took him. His absence was like an open wound. The pub was never the same without him; it felt hollow, the laughter quieter, the regulars a little more subdued.

At his funeral, the whole pub family turned up. Students, locals, our little group that once had to sit outside—everyone was there, filling the room with a silence that was more powerful than words. We hadn't just lost a landlord; we'd lost the father figure of our found family.

When I shifted to full-time at the computer company, the cash flow slowed down a bit, and my mate even offered Sarah and me a place to rent for cheap. It worked for a while, but we were all on top of each other. Eventually, I asked for a raise so I could get Sarah and me a place together, but they weren't budging.

Reading had become home—a proper community, especially among the Asian crowd who treated me like family. But reality was harsh. Living costs were sky high, and if they would not pay me more, I'd have to go. It wasn't easy. I'd made connections, memories, and friends for life. But I knew deep down that there was more out there waiting for me. So, with a heavy heart, I packed up and set off, knowing that one day, I'd look back on this time and remember it as one of the wildest, most formative periods of my life.

CHAPTER FIFTEEN

PROMISE IN MOTION

BUILDING MOMENTUM THROUGH PROMISES

I balanced boxes on the back seat and crammed bags into every corner, stuffing the car to the brim. I gripped the steering wheel, staring ahead at the road stretching into yet another unknown. Leaving behind the life and friends I'd fought hard to build, moving yet again—new town, fresh start, but the same gnawing fear of starting from scratch. It felt like I was on some endless carousel, always moving but getting nowhere. And yet, beneath the nerves, a promise stirred inside me, a quiet defiance that made my heart beat a little stronger. If I was leaving behind a life I'd fought to create, whatever came next had to be worth it. This time, I was going to make my life truly my own.

As I drove, a strange calm replaced the doubt. It was like fate was steering, guiding me toward the life I was meant to live. Maybe at 25, I was finally growing up. Experience had finally settled in, giving weight to the choices I made. This was no longer a kid's journey—I was taking on life headfirst, and for the first time, I knew what I wanted.

Back home, I sat down with my stepdad, hoping for a lead. "Do you think you could introduce me to your company?" I asked, trying to keep my voice steady. "Maybe they need someone with my skills."

He looked at me with a heavy sigh. "They're after qualifications, Scott," he said, almost apologetically. "You left your degree. Even if I could get a £6,000 bonus for an introduction, it wouldn't feel right."

It was like a slap to the face, a reminder of the cost of every decision I'd made. But I didn't argue—he was right, after all. I'd chosen my path. I sat there, swallowing the disappointment. The promise I'd made to myself, to Sarah, flickered in my mind like a beacon, steadying me, forcing me to keep going.

Fate still had more in store for me. That very afternoon, I spotted an ad in the paper. My stepdad's company was hiring Installation Engineers, and they'd won a major IT rollout contract. This was it—the perfect opportunity right under my nose.

Without a second thought, I headed straight to the company's open evening, joining a line that snaked through the building. The wait was agonising, but after two hours, I finally sat across from a recruitment consultant, my palms clammy and heart racing.

"You've got some skills," he began, "but not much experience..."

I cut in, determined to grab this chance. "Look, I'm a quick learner, and I've got the drive. Just give me a shot—I won't let you down."

He raised an eyebrow, clearly intrigued, and passed me on to another consultant, and then another. Each one threw a new test at me, a puzzle to solve, a challenge to tackle. I met each one head-on, feeling my confidence grow with each win.

They finally scheduled me for a full-day interview with the senior team. I walked into that room with my heart pounding, nerves on edge. "I'm not letting this slip away," I thought. "I've waited too long for this."

A week later, my phone rang with the news—I'd got the job. Decent salary, a brand-new company car, and the beginning of a new life I'd fought so hard for. It was everything I'd dreamed of, and yet, the moment it became real, fear started creeping in. Was I really ready for this?

The first day hit me hard. My stomach was in knots, every nerve buzzing with a mix of excitement and dread. But I'd made a promise to live without fear. I forced myself to walk through that door, head held high.

"Welcome to the team," a friendly voice greeted me as I walked in. "We're glad to have you on board."

The weeks that followed were relentless, filled with new lessons, long hours, and high stakes. I was saving every penny I could, planning for the future Sarah and I had talked about. We dreamed about our own place, a house that could be ours. Every moment, every challenge, felt worth it because I was finally building a life for myself.

Then we found it—our dream house, a three-bedroom tucked away in a quiet neighbourhood. Standing outside it together, hand in hand, it felt surreal, like a promise finally kept. We put down a deposit, securing a future that finally felt within reach.

Sarah found a job nearby as a food scientist, another piece of our dream falling into place. For the first time, I felt grounded, as if every setback, every struggle, had led to this moment.

> The promise I'd whispered to myself, the one that had driven me through every failure and every triumph, had finally come to life. I was creating the life I'd always wanted, with the woman I loved, and a future that stretched wide open before us.

Life was good. I'd finally found my place, and this time, I knew it was just the beginning. Whatever came next, I was ready.

CHAPTER SIXTEEN

PROMISES THROUGH THE WRECKAGE

THE STRENGTH OF PROMISES IN TOUGH TIMES

The house had the bare essentials: a bed, a couple of mismatched wicker chairs, and a scuffed-up dining table we'd inherited from Sarah's mum. But none of that mattered—we had each other, and for a while, that was everything. We laughed at our makeshift home, joked about our lack of furniture, and dreamed about the future we'd build within those walls. Life was simple, but we were happy.

Then Sarah had a car accident on her way to work, a shock that seemed to break something deeper inside her. She hated her job, and the accident only amplified her misery. When a position on the help desk opened up, I gently nudged her towards it, thinking a fresh start might lift her spirits. I did not know, though, how much our lives were about to change.

Meanwhile, I was thriving. Work on the road had paid off, and I landed a promotion to Implementation Manager. Suddenly, I was rolling out systems across the country, in charge, and enjoying the responsibility. I filled my weekends with wild Liverpool nights and my weekdays with building a career. The life I'd promised myself—success, stability, a career to be proud of—felt like it was finally coming together.

As my job progressed, the money flowed in, and piece by piece, the house transformed into a proper home. I even converted the garage, creating a space for my dream cinema setup and a DJ corner—a brief escape to my passions. Everything was going to plan, a life crafted from grit, dreams, and sheer hard work.

Then Sarah got pregnant, and our little boy arrived with a ferocious set of lungs and a serious case of colic. Nights became endless cycles of crying, feeding, and bouncing him around the house, trying anything to soothe him. We were exhausted, but utterly in love with our son. Two years later, our second boy arrived, calm and peaceful—a beautiful counterbalance to his older brother's lively chaos.

Parenthood was every bit as challenging as they say, but we were in it together, thick and thin. Mornings were a blur of routines, getting the boys ready, and rushing them to nursery. I would pick them up after work, both drained and content. Yet slowly, imperceptibly at first, something shifted.

Sarah started drinking, not in a way that screamed "problem" but enough to worry me. Her mum had battled with alcohol, and seeing Sarah slip into the same pattern was like watching a familiar shadow spread over our lives. I tried talking to her, suggesting we get help, but she brushed it off, the resentment simmering beneath the surface.

Friends drifted, family kept their distance. The arguments grew, her unhappiness seeped into every corner of our lives, and the woman I once knew seemed to disappear. I begged her to get help, to stop the cycle, but my words hit a wall. Each fight drained me, chipped away at the promise I'd made to build a good life for my family.

Then one night, everything imploded. Voices were raised, things were thrown, words that cut like knives. I stormed out, my heart pounding with a mix of anger and despair. The next morning, I returned, only to find her disoriented, barely remembering the fight. Something inside me broke that day. I couldn't do it anymore. I packed a bag, knowing that this time I was leaving for good.

The look on my boys' faces as I walked out felt like a knife to the chest. They were five and three, too young to fully understand, but old enough to feel the loss. Their innocent, questioning eyes haunted me as I closed the door, leaving behind a fractured family and a heart that felt shattered beyond repair.

I moved back in with my mum, feeling like a shell of the man I once was. I felt like I had been stripped of the confident, career-driven Scott, and left raw and exposed.

> But I made myself a new promise: "I will be there for my kids
> no matter what, and nothing will stand in my way."

Yet even this promise came with its own battle. Panic attacks started out of nowhere, gripping me with a terror I'd never known. Driving, something that had once been second nature, now left me paralysed. I would pull over, breathless, my heart racing, waiting for someone to come rescue me from my mind.

Every Thursday, I'd pick up my boys, driving an hour back to my mum's house. Those journeys were agony. Panic clawed at me, my hands gripped the wheel, and tears often blurred my vision. My heart would pound, my arms would go numb, and my mind screamed at me to turn back. But I'd made a promise, and that promise was my lifeline.

"Keep going," I'd whisper to myself. "You can't let the boys down." Each mile was a test of willpower, a battle against fear, but I fought it for them. My sons deserved a dad who showed up, who loved them fiercely, and who would never, ever give up on them.

Slowly, painfully, I rebuilt. That promise to my boys—to be there, to fight through the fear—kept me moving forward. It wasn't easy, and it wasn't pretty, but I found the strength to carry on, one step, one drive, one tear-filled promise at a time. For them. For myself. For a future I still believed in, no matter how far it seemed.

CHAPTER SEVENTEEN

BACK TO SQUARE ONE

FINDING STRENGTH IN NEW BEGINNINGS

Moving back with Mum was like landing on a safe shore after being lost at sea. I never thought I'd be back, but after Sarah took just about everything in the divorce – the house, the furniture, even the bloody toaster – there wasn't much left for me but a suitcase and some pride. Mum's place felt like the last place I'd be staying, at this stage of my life, but I didn't have a choice. It was humbling, but there was a spark in me that wouldn't let me settle.

As I unpacked, I glanced at the faces of my two boys. They did not know how much had fallen apart, and I intended to keep it that way. I made a promise to them, and to myself: I'll rebuild from this, and I'll make you proud. It was a big promise, maybe the hardest I'd made yet, but it anchored me in a way nothing else could.

For now, we took over Mum's house with a whirlwind of noise. The boys — young, innocent, and full of energy — kept my days far too busy for wallowing. Mum and my stepdad, who were used to a quieter life, suddenly found themselves caught up in our chaos. I'd take the boys out as much as I could, to give Mum a break and so they could see that, no matter what, their dad was there for them.

Over time, I started feeling the need for adult company. No grand romance, just someone to talk to, someone who wasn't asking me for snack breaks or bedtime stories. So, I did what any single dad might do – I dipped a toe in the world of online dating.

This journey took me to some interesting places. There was the woman who insisted I drive her to Blackpool for chips because her last boyfriend said no. I actually went through with it, just for the story, but it's safe to say it didn't last. Then I met Jenny on a site called Country Lovers, and this time, things clicked.

Jenny was incredible. She didn't seem phased by my past, and she wasn't trying to fix me. She was a breath of fresh air – just what I needed to move forward. With her, I found a calm space to heal. Jenny had her own little house and a small dog named Tess, and before I knew it, we were planning a future together.

Nine months later, with my debts finally paid off, Jenny and I moved into a cosy farmhouse. We bought home a new puppy, Honey, and my life felt like it was finding balance again. But just as things started feeling right, Tess's eye problems began. The vet said there was pressure behind one eye that needed surgery, and, incredibly, Tess adapted. Then the same thing happened to her other eye, and we had a tough choice – leave her sightless or put her down. We chose surgery, but if she couldn't cope, we'd make the hard call.

But Tess thrived. That little dog, stumbling around but happy as anything, taught me a lesson in resilience I'd never forget. Watching her adapt reminded me of my journey – if she could find her way, so could I.

Life ticked along nicely after that. We were ready to buy our own place, and I was finally going to get my DJ decks back in action. But life, always one to surprise, had other plans. Driving early one morning, a van that sent my car spinning blindsided me. I remember everything slowing down; the van slamming into my driver's side, and the memories of my old driving anxiety came flooding back.

Jenny insisted I get back in the car the same day, but the fear gnawed at me. The panic attacks, which I'd thought I'd left behind, came back stronger. Each time I took the wheel, it was a battle, but I kept going – for the boys, for Jenny, and for that promise I'd made. We realised it was time for a new start, so we moved closer to the boys, to somewhere Jenny could keep her horses, and to a fresh chapter that had yet to be written.

This wasn't the life I'd planned, but as I looked ahead, I knew one thing: the promise to myself, and to the people I loved, was worth every battle I'd face.

CHAPTER EIGHTEEN

PROMISES THROUGH DISTANCE AND DARKNESS

UNBROKEN BONDS

Jenny and I had just moved into our dream home—a huge white house with stables and land, set against the rolling countryside outside Shrewsbury. It felt like a fresh start, where memories are made. Best of all, we were only ten minutes from the boys. I could work remotely, with the occasional trip to the office. Life felt like it was finally falling into place.

Then, two weeks in, Sarah dropped a bombshell. She called me, voice cold and matter-of-fact.

"I'm moving with the boys," she said.

I paused, caught off-guard. "Moving where?"

"Over a hundred miles away, with Dave, we want to be a family. It'll be better for them," she added, as if that made everything fine.

My mind reeled. "Sarah, that's two and a half hours each way. You know I struggle with driving. How am I supposed to see them?"

She didn't miss a beat. "You'll just have to work it out. They'll settle in fine, don't worry."

I felt the weight of it settle like a lead weight in my chest. "That's easy for you to say, Sarah," I replied, my voice cracking. "You're the one taking them away, but I promised them I'd always be there."

She gave a dismissive sigh, the finality of her decision clear. "It's done, Scott. They're coming with me."

The call ended, and the silence felt like it was crushing me. Suddenly, that promise I'd clung to—that I'd always be there for my boys—felt like a cruel joke.

I could barely drive twenty minutes without feeling panic clawing at my throat, let alone make a five-hour round trip. The darkness of self-doubt and guilt flooded in, relentless. Those familiar, taunting whispers: *You're not good enough. You've failed them. They deserve better.*

I made a dozen attempts to drive to them. Each time, the anxiety took over. I'd pull over to the side of the road, gripping the wheel until my knuckles were white, tears streaming down my face. Guilt was eating away at me. The boys needed me, and here I was, crippled by a fear I couldn't control. The shame was unbearable. Those darker thoughts I'd buried started creeping back. *Maybe it's better if you just disappear. You're useless to them, anyway.*

It got so bad that I ended up at the doctor's office, seeking something, anything, to quiet my mind. The medication helped to dull the constant barrage of self-doubt, but I knew I wasn't out of the woods. I had to accept what I couldn't change, that Sarah had made this choice, and she would have to bring the boys to me when possible.

She agreed, begrudgingly, but only on her terms—a few times a year. An ache that couldn't be filled was caused by each goodbye. I'd come home, stare at the empty house, and feel the hollow space they left behind.

Through all of this, Jenny was my anchor, never wavering. She listened when I needed to vent, held me when the weight was too much, and kept me steady when everything else felt like it was falling apart. So, I did what felt right. I asked her to marry me. She'd been my rock, and I wanted to make our commitment official. We formed a team, and I knew I couldn't do it without her.

Marriage gave us something to look forward to, and I threw myself into building something stable for us. I started a website SEO business, pouring my energy into making it a success. For a while, things were looking up; we were saving for our own home, watching the deposit slowly grow. But just as I felt we were making progress, someone suddenly pulled the rug out from under me. My business partner betrayed me, siphoning money from a client, and then hackers tore through my site, deleting everything. Months of work, wiped out in an instant.

> The frustration was overwhelming. It felt like every time I got a foothold, life knocked me back down. But I had to keep going, for Jenny, for the boys, for myself.

Then we tried for a baby. It felt like the right time. With the boys so far away, having another child to focus on gave me a renewed sense of purpose.

But life had one more twist in store. During a routine check-up, the doctor kept Jenny in. Her blood pressure was dangerously high, and the doctors diagnosed her with HELLP syndrome—a rare and severe complication that could threaten both her life and our baby's. I remember sitting beside her hospital bed, watching her, terrified, as they explained the risks. Our baby girl was lying in the wrong position, and a natural birth was impossible. They would have to rush Jenny into surgery.

They wheeled her out, and I found myself alone in that sterile waiting room, each second feeling like an eternity. Finally, a nurse appeared, cradling my tiny daughter. She was perfect, with a little red heart-shaped mark on her forehead. My heart swelled with relief and joy as I held her close, but it was bittersweet.

"What about Jenny?" I asked, a lump forming in my throat.

The nurse hesitated. "She's had complications, but she's stable. She's not awake yet."

As I held my daughter, I couldn't stop the tears. I'd waited so long for this moment, but the fear of losing Jenny marred the joy. The nurse finally wheeled her in, barely conscious, hooked up to a ventilator. It broke me to see her like that, our family together but fragile, as if it could shatter at any moment.

That night, they told me I couldn't stay. I begged to be allowed to remain by their side, but the staff insisted. As I walked out, leaving my daughter in an incubator and Jenny barely clinging to consciousness, I felt hollow.

The next day, a snowstorm hit. I spent hours shovelling snow; the cold numbing my fingers, the harsh wind biting at my face. It felt like the universe was piling on one more obstacle, testing how much I could endure. But somehow, I found a strange sense of calm amid it all. If that storm had come a day earlier, the ambulance might not have made it in time. Jenny and my daughter might not have made it. It was a brutal reminder of how close we'd come, and how precious every moment was.

A week later, on the due date, Jenny came home. Our little family was together again, fragile but intact. The snow-covered landscape outside our window served as a symbol of everything we'd been through—a hard, cold season that, somehow, we'd survived.

Life kept throwing its punches, but I'd made a promise to weather every storm, to be there no matter how difficult things got. Holding my daughter, watching Jenny finally sleep peacefully, I felt something I hadn't in a long time: hope.

CHAPTER NINETEEN

AGAINST ALL ODDS

BUILDING DREAMS AND BATTLING SETBACKS

Our little girl was growing fast, full of energy and wonder, and I couldn't have been prouder. We'd finally saved up enough for a deposit, enough to make the jump to a place of our own. Every day, I'd spend thirty minutes with my "mind machine," visualising exactly what I wanted: an old, beautiful house with a glass front, a stunning view, stables for Jenny's horses, and enough space for me to work from home.

Jenny and I started our search, but we found that everything we viewed was not quite right or someone would snap it up before we could even view them. The market was hot. Then we stumbled upon this house in Wales. I'll never forget seeing it for the first time—it ticked every box. A cosy two-bedroom with a second-floor conservatory, a barn (albeit uninsulated), four acres, a bit of woodland, and its own stream. Perfect. Or so I thought.

Jenny, ever the pragmatist, had her reservations. "The land's too steep for the horses," she pointed out. "And our daughter's bedroom is a bit too far from ours."

"Really?" I muttered, crestfallen, though I knew she was right. We both needed to love it, and it wasn't fair to push her.

So, we kept looking. But a few weeks later, Jenny turned to me and said, "Should we go back and look at that place in Wales?"

My heart leapt. We went for a second look, and she compromised. The next thing we knew, the house was ours.

The move felt like a win. My hours spent visualising that dream house had somehow manifested it—well, with a fair bit of hard work along the way. We had stables built, and I set up the barn with carpet and a log burner, turning one side into a makeshift gym and the other into my office. Life finally felt like it was clicking into place.

It was summer when we moved in, and it was bliss. Honey and Tess, our dogs, loved the freedom, darting across the open fields. Jenny, our daughter Maisie, and I were settling into a new rhythm. For once, everything was working out.

Then, just as Maisie turned two, the phone rang. It was my boss.

"Scott, I'm so sorry," he began, voice cracking as he tried to keep it together. "This is really hard for me to say...after seventeen years with the company, we're letting you go."

Seventeen years. Almost two decades poured into this company. In that time, I'd climbed the ladder rung by rung, pushing past obstacles and taking on challenges, stretching myself to every limit. I'd built a career here from the ground up, one promotion after another, all earned through grit, long hours, and the drive to excel. I'd travelled the world with them—new cities, new cultures, all in the name of building something that I believed was mine too.

Across Europe, I'd handpicked and built teams, coached and mentored people from the starting line to leadership, even had to make the hard calls, hiring and firing to keep the business moving. It felt like a living thing, something I'd nurtured and grown with, and every minor success, every challenge overcome, felt like a testament to what I could do.

Throughout my time managing over twenty-five people across Europe, each with their own goals, quirks, and strengths, I guided them through project after project, delivering results I believed spoke for themselves. I'd believed my impact was deep-rooted and that I'd earned my place not just as a manager but as a proper leader. I thought I was irreplaceable, that after nearly two decades of giving it everything, I'd secured my position, my future, with the company.

But here I stood, with the phone pressed to my ear, as I heard him summing up those seventeen years—all the highs, the lows, the all-nighters, the countless airports, and hotel rooms—all gone in that short, impossible phrase, "We're letting you go."

I sat there, stunned. "Wait, what?" I finally managed.

He continued, stumbling over his words. I comforted him, not fully grasping the reality that I'd just lost my job.

Hanging up, I went to Jenny. "They've let me go," I said, half in disbelief.

She put her hand on my shoulder, steady as ever. "We'll get through it," she assured me. "We always do."

Months passed in a blur of CVs, interviews, and near-misses. Every job seemed to slip through my fingers. The market had shifted, with openings for "doers," not managers. I felt stuck, wondering if my experience meant anything at all. My confidence took a dive, and I became distant. Jenny noticed, questioning why I was struggling to find work.

It didn't help that I was at home with Maisie, juggling job-hunting and keeping her entertained. Each rejection hit harder, and I felt the weight of worthlessness creeping in. Jenny doubted my efforts, thinking I was wasting my time in the barn. Tension built, and it tested us both in ways we hadn't expected.

Just as we were about to hit rock bottom, with only a month's worth of money left, I landed a consultancy role. It was a relief beyond words. But since I was new to contracting, I went with an umbrella company that the prime contractor recommended. The pay was good—almost suspiciously good—but I didn't question it. My focus was on rebuilding my confidence, not on tax logistics. More on that nightmare with the taxman later.

The contract was supposed to last six months, but we wrapped up early in four. Suddenly, I found myself out of work again. The frustration was unbearable. Was I jinxed or something?

Then, a few months later, a recruiter called with a role that seemed tailor-made for me. "There's a presentation component," she mentioned, "and it's in London."

> I took a deep breath, reminding myself of my promise: no fear, no backing down. I needed this job, and everything depended on it.

On the day I got on the train to London, nerves bubbling under the surface. I chatted with the receptionist on arrival, trying to keep calm, until the interviewer came to fetch me. Inside the office, five faces watched as I began my presentation. I took a breath, remembered my promise, and went for it. I nailed it.

Walking out, I felt pride swell up inside me. Even if I didn't get the job, I'd held my ground. I'd proven to myself that I could still deliver under pressure.

The call came as I was on my way home. "They loved you," the recruiter said, and they agreed to a salary double what I'd earned before. It was the validation I'd been craving.

When I got home, I told Jenny, and we celebrated, both of us overwhelmed with relief. It had been a tough road, but finally, it felt like we were moving forward.

A new chapter was on the horizon, and this time, I was ready.

Chapter Twenty

RUNNING THE GAUNTLET

PROJECT X AND THE HIGHS AND LOWS OF LIFE IN LONDON

Just a week into my new job, and another unexpected challenge hit me. My new manager rang me up out of nowhere. "Scott, we're going to need you in London full time," he said, as casually as if he were asking me to pick up a pint on the way home. London? 120 miles away? Maisie was only two, and I felt a pang of guilt hit hard. I imagined Jenny's face, already stressed with the daily chaos of raising a toddler, and here I was about to tell her she'd be handling it alone four days a week.

I braced myself for that conversation. "Look, it's an enormous opportunity, and we need it," I said, trying to keep my voice steady. Jenny looked at me, half understanding, half exasperated. She nodded, but the strain was already visible.

At least I could take the train. That first morning, I sat in a packed carriage with a coffee in hand, feeling half-optimistic, half-sick with nerves. Walking into the office that day, I was like a deer caught in headlights. My new manager showed me the ropes and warned me of one thing: "Don't touch Project X. It's off-limits—it conflicts with our major work." With that, he was off on holiday, leaving me to get on with it.

So there I was, head down, working hard, getting to know the team. A few days in, I'm called into a meeting, and the Programme Director pops by. "You seem to know what you're talking about," he says, raising an eyebrow. "I'd like you to take over Project X." I nearly laughed out loud, but he wasn't joking. I'd been there less than a week! Still, he was insistent. I tried suggesting that he clear it with my manager first, but he brushed it off, and just like that, he put me in charge of the very project I'd been warned to stay away from.

When my manager got back and found out, he lost it. Right there, in front of the client, he laid into me. I was getting an earful, and all I could think was, *This can't be real.* Thankfully, the client wasn't too impressed with his outburst and asked for him to be removed from the meeting. But, with twenty years at the company under his belt, he had sway. Word spread, and I started noticing people giving me the cold shoulder, distancing themselves.

No time for it, though—I had a £12 million project to deliver. I pulled together a team of forty-five and threw myself into it. Pressure? You have no idea. Every day, it felt like a fresh crisis hit, and every time, I leaned on that old promise to push through anything. The client demanded a lot. My team was exhausted, but somehow, we kept it moving.

After a few months, my team insisted I join them at their hotel instead of staying on my own. At first, it seemed like a great way to bond, so I booked in. My mate Pete was there too, and we started a routine that quickly got out of hand—three-course dinners, eight pints, late nights. I'd missed a call home here and there, too, lost in the haze of meetings and pints. And I noticed a few more inches on my waistline.

Back home, Jenny wasn't thrilled. She was stuck with Maisie, exhausted and feeling abandoned while I was off living a London life. I'd get home on Thursdays, armed with flowers, a tired smile, and treats for Maisie, but I could tell it wasn't enough. She'd just hand me the reins and vanish on her horse, craving her own escape. The tension simmered.

Health-wise, things weren't much better. Too many hours hunched over a desk, too many missed gym sessions, and my knees were practically shouting at me. Then, they brought in a new Project Director. She was keen to make a name for herself, and from day one, it felt like she had her sights set on making my life hell. I'd built a solid team, people who trusted me, but she was stirring the pot, questioning my every move.

The stress was piling on, and I could feel the burn. This wasn't just a job anymore—it was survival. I kept reminding myself of that promise: *I've handled worse; I can handle this.* But deep down, I wondered, *How long can I keep this up?*

CHAPTER TWENTY-ONE

TURNING POINT

WHEN EVERYTHING CRUMBLED

Monday morning, I walked into the office, half-asleep and already counting down the hours to Friday. But the new Project Director was waiting for me, a look on her face that made my stomach sink. "Scott, my office. Now," she barked, barely giving me a chance to put my bag down. The door closed with a slam, and she went straight into a tirade, asking question after question about the project, drilling me like I was some rookie.

"Is this going to be delivered on time?" she pressed, her tone sharp.

"Yes, absolutely. We're on it," I assured her, trying to keep my composure. "Look, my team and I have handled this with no fuss, no fluff. Just five of us doing the work of ten, and we're committed to getting it done."

She stared me down, the silence heavy. Then, with cold eyes, she leaned in and hissed, "You'd better."

This wasn't just pressure anymore; it was like standing in the middle of a storm with no shelter in sight. Our team was deploying critical IT systems into UK Court offices. One wrong move, and we'd bring the whole thing down, causing chaos. We gave her all the reports she demanded, but it never seemed enough. Week after week, she'd pull me into her office, scrutinising every detail, convinced we were heading for disaster. It felt less like a job and more like a siege.

One day, she crossed a line. "Listen, Scott," she said, practically locking the door behind me. "Richard's leaving, which means I'm in charge. You'll be reporting directly to me now. Either get on board with that, or... don't. Make your decision."

That was it. I'd had enough. I decided after leaving her office, grabbing a pint with my team to vent, and made up my mind. I would not put up with this. After all the hard work, dedication, and effort I put in for eighteen months, all I received was her bullying. I told the team, "I'm heading home. I need a break, and I'm not sticking around to be someone's doormat."

That night, I stayed over in London, but I was on the first train out at 5:30 a.m. The thought of heading home to Jenny and Maisie gave me some sense of peace, like maybe I'd left all that rubbish behind for good. I filled Jenny in on what had happened, and as soon as I walked in, I gave her a kiss, told her I was off to see the doctor, and promised I'd be back soon.

At the doctor's, I poured everything out—the pressure, the constant scrutiny, the sheer exhaustion. He didn't hesitate. "Scott, you're burned out," he said, handing me a note for two weeks' sick leave. I felt a wave of relief. Finally, I had permission to take a breath.

I got home, ready to tell Jenny I'd be around for a bit to get my head straight. But she had a different plan. She looked at me, her gaze firm but with a glint of something I couldn't read. "I don't want you here anymore," she said, her voice barely a whisper. "I think it's time you went back to London."

"What?" I stammered, completely blindsided. "What are you saying?"

"I don't love you anymore, Scott. I want you to leave."

It hit like a punch to the face again. I stared at her, waiting for her to take it back, to say something that would make sense. But she didn't. She just stood there, resolute, and I knew she meant every word.

Heart pounding, I grabbed my suitcase, threw in what I could, and headed to my mum's. For the weekend, I stayed there, hoping that Jenny would change her mind, that maybe this was just a blip. But when I went back, she made it clear again. "You're a good man, Scott, and a brilliant father. But this isn't working. It's over."

It was like everything was crumbling at once. I'd barely come up for air from work, and now my marriage, my fami-ly—everything I'd been holding onto—was slipping away. "But why?" I asked, almost pleading. "What can I do?"

"Nothing," she said, her voice soft but unwavering. "It's done."

In a daze, I moved my things into the barn. My life had turned upside down, and I was a mess. I'd go days barely functioning, the weight of it all pressing down so hard I thought I'd break. The next morning, I went back to the doctor, told him everything. He didn't even blink, just signed me off for three months, telling me to sort my life out.

So there I was. The dreams of a happy family, of raising Maisie every day, of being a part of her life—all gone in a flash. I sat alone in that barn, looking around at the wreckage of my life, asking myself one question: *What the hell am I going to do now?*

CHAPTER TWENTY-TWO

LIVING IN THE BARN

LETTING GO AND MOVING FORWARD

Living in the barn was a mix of comfort and heartbreak. Through that little window, I could see Jenny, sitting in the conservatory, surrounded by everything we'd built together—the life I was now shut out from. Every time I glimpsed her, I felt a surge to walk over, to ask her one more time if there was a chance. But each time I tried, she'd look right through me with that same empty expression.

"It's over, Scott. Accept it," she'd say, as if repeating it could make it easier for either of us. I'd stand there, grasping for anything that might change her mind. "So... what do we do then?" I finally asked one day, my voice flat.

She sighed. "Go back to work in London if you need to. You can keep the barn on weekends if you want it."

The barn was my escape, a place where I'd carved out a bit of my own. It had everything I loved: a mini gym, pool table, dartboard, my projector. But it wasn't where I wanted to spend my life, hiding out alone every weekend, half-living. I knew Jenny too well to misread her eyes. She'd checked out. For her, I was a chapter closed.

With a heavy heart, I trudged back to the barn, my head spinning. What did this mean for me? For Maisie? I rang my dad, searching for some kind of anchor. "Son," he said after listening patiently, "don't lose the house this time. It took you years to build this up. Don't let it go so easily." He was right. I couldn't just walk away from everything again.

I started looking at other options and found a small cottage listed nearby. It was quaint, just right for Jenny and Maisie, and close enough that I could still see Maisie regularly. I asked Jenny if that's what she wanted, and she said yes, without hesitation. So, I re-mortgaged the house, put down the deposit, and got her set up.

The weeks that followed felt surreal. I'd pick up Maisie after school, help with her tea, and then retreat to the barn to let the emptiness take over. The silence became an unbearable weight, pressing down with every passing night. I stopped talking to people, even avoiding my family. Instead, I turned to walking. Three hours every day, through the hills and winding paths, letting the rhythm of my steps drown out the noise in my head.

It was on those long walks that the fog lifted, just a little. I had to stop blaming Jenny, even though she never really told me why. Deep down, I knew. I'd become someone she couldn't reach anymore, a person on a different path from hers. When I stopped asking questions, the answers finally started to take shape.

Walking led to training. I threw myself into boxing, lifting weights, chopping logs until my arms were sore. The weight dropped off me, and I looked different, like someone with a new strength. But even then, I couldn't shake the quiet hope that maybe Jenny would notice. She didn't. She was done. And I'd just have to accept that.

Life in the barn became routine, the quiet only broken by little intrusions—cats dropping off their "gifts" of dead mice in the middle of the night or the creaking roof that seemed to come alive just as I was falling asleep. But in that strange quiet, I found a new peace. Nights alone, no answers in sight, yet somehow, a clarity was settling in.

A couple of months later, Jenny moved into the cottage. But there was a catch: no place to keep her horses. She asked to keep them at the house, which meant twice a day she'd come back to take care of them. I knew every time her car pulled up, I'd feel that tug again, that sliver of hope that maybe we'd get back to who we once were.

But she kept her distance, each encounter a painful reminder that I was clinging to something gone. "It's over, Scott. I live in a different house now," she'd say. And that's when it hit me: I was chasing a ghost. This wasn't about her anymore. It was about me, facing the space I was too afraid to fill.

Then the phone rang. My boss needed me in Norwich—on Monday. Norwich. I couldn't think of a place further away if I tried. Five and a half hours on the train, every week just to get there. But the bills would not pay themselves, and I had to keep things together. So I packed my bag, boarded that train, and let the next chapter begin, hoping I'd finally learned to make peace with the past.

CHAPTER TWENTY-THREE

HEALING, MISSTEPS, AND A HOLIDAY REMINDER

Going to Norwich felt like a new chapter, though my confidence was shaky. I hadn't been at work in three months, and the thought of explaining my absence made me uneasy.

But I'd made a promise to rebuild my life, so I pushed myself back into the grind.

I started a disciplined routine—up at five a.m. for a hard workout, a brisk hour-long walk to the office in the early morning sun. It wasn't like the hills of Wales, but it was something. After work, I'd stroll back, pick up some food from Marks and Spencer, and settle into my quiet hotel room. To keep the loneliness at bay, I threw myself into evening yoga classes, followed by an hour-long swim. By the time I got back, exhaustion had set in enough for me to fall asleep without my mind churning.

With time on my hands, I dipped into dating apps for some company. Met a few interesting people, but they weren't what I was looking for. Deep down, I knew I wasn't healed yet. After a few light-hearted but unfulfilling dates, I knocked it on the head. For now, I'd keep focusing on myself.

Maisie was my beacon through all of this. Every other Friday, I'd catch the train home, brimming with excitement to see her. Her smile, her hugs—those were the moments that held me together. One weekend, I booked a family holiday, something we'd never really had before. I'd finally saved up enough, so I arranged for a little cottage in Tenby with a pool and some nearby football fields for the boys. I couldn't wait to give them this memory.

That weekend, I was meant to go to a friend's 50th birthday party, but the stress of the week had me itching for fresh air. I dusted off my bike, ready to hit the Welsh hills for a quick ride. And in true "me" fashion, I thought, "Maybe I'll wear a helmet today—better safe than sorry." Smart move.

I hadn't even hit the last hill when the weather turned on me. One minute it was clear, and the next, rain poured down like it was auditioning for a monsoon. Then, a flash of lightning struck nearby. I sped up, but the bike started wobbling—next thing I knew, I was airborne, head first into the ground at twenty-five mph. My chin hit the road, and as I got up, I noticed my wrist looked more like a banana than a bone.

Stumbling home, dripping wet and bloodied, I called Jenny. "Any chance you could pick me up?" I mumbled, the shock setting in.

"No, sorry," she replied, her voice cool. I felt the familiar sting of disappointment but dialled for an ambulance, staying conscious long enough to answer the EMTs' questions as they clumsily banged my stretcher around. Morphine helped, but I was ready to pass out just from the chaos.

After a few hours and a fair bit of NHS magic, I came out of surgery with my wrist newly pieced together. The next day, Dad picked me up, bringing me home, where I wrestled with daily tasks. Changing a duvet cover with one hand? Absolute nightmare. But, on the bright side, my son came to stay for a bit during the holidays, bringing a lightness I desperately needed. We'd wander down to the pub, chat, and bond over home-cooked meals—he even took on the task of debating why I wasn't ready to meet someone new yet.

Finally, it was time for the Tenby holiday. With my wrist still mending, I couldn't drive, but my stepdad offered to take the wheel. We had a brilliant time—hopping on buses, walking everywhere, soaking up the sun and the sea. Watching the kids roughhouse in the water, my promise to them felt as vivid as ever. They were my world, and moments like these reminded me why I kept going.

On the last day, while they played, I found a quiet bench, basking in the afternoon sun. A thought crept in—what if I could share this life with someone who felt right? Someone who could fit into this picture.

> Pulling out my phone, I opened the dating app again, this time with a clear vision of what I wanted. I sent a message to a woman who seemed interesting, figuring I'd see where things went when we got back.

Once the kids returned to their mum's, the silence set in again. The house was empty, and with that quiet came the familiar pang of loneliness. So, I sat down and wrote out exactly what I wanted out of life—a new beginning, a meaningful relationship, and a purpose that would keep me grounded. With Maisie's and the boys' laughter still fresh in my memory, a new chapter unfolded.

CHAPTER TWENTY-FOUR

THE LIST, A LEAP OF FAITH

WONDER WOMAN

After six weeks signed off work to heal, I was climbing the walls with boredom. I needed something, anything, to fill my time. So, I figured I'd share my journey, blog-style—talk about the divorce, the small steps I'd taken to move forward, maybe throw in a few videos. I thought, *Who's going to care?* But, turns out, people did. Comments poured in: "Scott, you're such an inspiration! How do you do it? How can I follow your path?"

It floored me. I'd always had an itch to help others, maybe coach them through tough times, but my mates had always shrugged it off as "Scott, going on about his self-help stuff is boring mate, pack it in." But this time was different. The positive feedback was like fuel; people actually valued what I had to say. So, I leaned in, trained as a Transformation Coach, even studied the Three Principles. My passion was on fire.

One evening, I poured a glass of wine, sat down with my notepad, and got real with myself. I asked myself a few big questions:

- What do I *really* want in life?

- Who do I want by my side, and what will they be like?

- How can I support my kids, spare them some of the pain I've known?

- What would my dream life look like?

With these thoughts swirling around, I got specific. I wanted a partner who was funny, kind, loved children, took care of herself, and—most importantly—loved me for *me*. She'd have to look after herself, be able to say sorry, and look...well, a bit like Wonder Woman wouldn't hurt. It might have sounded ridiculous, but I figured, *Why not?*

Night after night, I visualised her. I could feel it, like she was already there, laughing with me, building a life with me. And one night, as I was deep in my usual routine, my phone pinged.

It was the lady I'd messaged on the dating app while on holiday. Her reply was kind, warm. She said, "Your message was lovely. You sound really nice—would you like to chat?" I was buzzing. The blog and feedback had brought my confidence back, so I texted her, and before long, we were laughing on WhatsApp, the conversation flowing like we'd known each other for years.

Since I couldn't drive yet, it was just calls at first. But when the cast finally came off, and my wrist healed, we set a date.

We chose a cosy little pub in Shropshire. I spotted her in the car park, and my heart skipped a beat. *Wow!* Abi got out of the car, eyes glistening, her smile as wide as mine. We spent an hour laughing, just being real with each other, and when she turned to leave, she paused, came back, kissed me softly, and said, "What a lovely time I've had."

I floated home, called my mum, and practically shouted down the phone, "Mum, she's amazing!"

"Take it easy, Scott," she chuckled. "Early days!"

> But I'd never felt this way before. Was this love at first sight? I didn't know, but I texted Abi as soon as I got home: *"Would love to see you again—would you?"* She replied, *"Yes, I'd like that."*

Our second date couldn't come fast enough. We talked about everything, from past relationships to our quirks. It was honest, raw. When I told her I'd been married twice, I could feel her weighing my words. But she was open too; she'd been married once, and her daughter Polly had no relationship with her dad.

Then, out of nowhere, Abi laughed. "I have a confession. I'm actually turning fifty this weekend. I, uh...might've lied on the app." She smirked. "I was looking for someone younger, someone ambitious."

I laughed, "You know, age is just a number. And you're stunning—so no harm done." Her twinkling eyes had me completely mesmerised.

For our third date, though, things took an unexpected turn. I'd just gotten back to work, working from home instead of Norwich, when my phone pinged.

"Scott, I'm so sorry, but I can't go through with this," she'd written. *"I wasn't looking for a relationship, just some company. But I'm falling for you too quickly, and I need to end it before it gets harder."*

My heart sank. I replied, "I understand, Abi. I think you're incredible, and I'll be here if you ever change your mind." I meant it.

A few days later, she was texting again, saying she'd stumbled upon my blog and read through the comments. She'd even watched my videos, and it helped her see I was genuine. The weekend was a rollercoaster of texts and calls, and finally, she said, *I want to be with you. Can we meet up?*

When I saw her again, I told her about my list, about manifesting Wonder Woman, and we had a good laugh. Then Abi pulled her keys from her bag and held them up—a Wonder Woman keyring dangled there.

"Well, that's a sign if ever I saw one," I said, smiling.

We both knew this was special. It felt like fate was drawing us together; the universe nudging us closer. And for the first time in a long time, I knew I was heading towards something amazing, a new set of promises. This new chapter, I promised myself, would be everything I'd ever dreamed of—and more.

Chapter Twenty-Five

THE MISSING PIECE

Making Promises Real

Abi and I moved forward together in sync, as if it were always meant to be. Our kids had met, and everyone was getting along brilliantly, more or less. Polly and Maisie were an interesting combo—a fifteen-year-old and a five-year-old. They had that playful push-pull relationship, but it warmed my heart to see them bonding in their own way.

Even though I stayed at Abi's place a couple of nights a week, it wasn't enough. I wanted to be with her full-time, to create something lasting. So, I started looking for houses near Abi's place. Polly was in school, and we didn't want to disrupt her studies, and Maisie was only a short drive away. Moving closer just made sense.

I was determined to find our place, even though nothing seemed quite right at first. The decision to leave the farmhouse and my beloved barn wasn't easy; it was more than just walls and a roof. But I'd found what I truly wanted with Abi. I found a buyer quickly—someone who had big plans for the old place—and with the farmhouse sale moving forward, Abi and I began the search for something that would fit us all.

Then one day, a new house came on the market. Despite not being fully finished, they had opened up the show home, so we went along for a peek. The moment we walked in, Abi and I exchanged a look—it was perfect. Open-plan downstairs, which meant plenty of family space, four bedrooms, a charming little village, and, as luck would have it, a bus stop right outside for Polly's school run.

"This is the one," I said, feeling it in my bones. I made the call, agreed to the sale, and just like that, we had our new home lined up. While we waited for the house to be ready, I moved in with Abi and Polly temporarily, and all my stuff went into the garage. Leaving the farmhouse was bittersweet, like closing the door on a past chapter, but it felt right. This was our new start.

A couple of months later, the house was ready. My dad came over to lend a hand, and Abi and I had a blast getting everything we needed. New sofas, wardrobes, a dining table—all the bits and pieces that made it feel like our own. Moving in, it all felt like the beginning of something wonderful.

Life settled beautifully. My divorce finally came through, giving me the closure I didn't even realise I was waiting for. Jenny and I got along well enough, and I had Maisie every other weekend, plus extra whenever I could. She fit right in with Abi, Polly, and me. The boys came over for family barbecues, walks, and even a few holidays. I'd sit back and watch it all sometimes, thinking, *This is it. This is the family I'd always wanted and promised myself I would get.*

Then, as if it were the most natural thing in the world, I proposed. Abi and I joked about it afterward—she calls herself

"Mrs Adams the 3rd" for a laugh. That's Abi for you, always finding a way to make us smile.

We started the hunt for wedding venues, but nothing quite captured us. Then we came across a place right on the Welsh border. It was an old barn with a beautiful modern twist. Immaculate and stunning, it was exactly what we'd been dreaming of. Abi did the classic "wedding venue test," marching into the toilets and checking everything out. When she gave it her seal of approval, I thought, *Right, this is it!*

Then we looked at the prices. My heart sank—they wanted half the payment upfront, and it was just too much. Disappointment hung heavy over us, and on the way home, we agreed to take a step back, let it simmer, and see what other options might come up.

Later, I called the venue and explained our situation to the lady who managed the place. "If you receive any cancellations or last-minute openings," I told her, "we would be thrilled to take them."

Life continued on, like it was guiding us towards something amazing, but that perfect wedding venue still felt out of reach. We were gutted, not sure if our dream wedding would happen there.

And then, one afternoon, the phone rang...

CHAPTER TWENTY-SIX

A TWIST OF FATE

THE WEDDING WAS ON

The call came out of the blue. It was the lady from the wedding venue. "I don't know if you'd be interested," she said, "but we're testing a special fixed-price package for next March. Would that work for you?" She went through the details and pricing, and it was half what we'd initially expected. My heart pounded—I told her I'd speak to Abi first.

I phoned Abi, barely able to contain my excitement. "Guess what?" I asked, practically bouncing through the line. When I explained, she was over the moon, laughing with a big "Yes, yes, yes!" It was like the universe had aligned just for us.

The deposit was low, and we'd pay the rest closer to the date. It felt like everything was falling into place; after all the waiting and hoping, here it was, our wedding, right around the corner. We jumped into planning mode, piecing together every detail.

But just as the excitement was building, the job was weighing on me. After everything—the bullying, the broken wrist, the endless travel to Norwich—I was ready to let go of that chapter. I'd started a coaching business, but I knew it would take time to establish. I handed in my notice, trusting that something would come through.

And then the phone rang again. It was a recruitment agency with a six-month contract for a major IT supplier—a project that would cover the wedding costs and give us the stability we needed. It felt surreal. I was on a roll, as if the universe was giving us everything we'd asked for yet again. Working from home with the occasional travel to Europe was a bonus, making it feel worlds away from the stress of my previous job.

Then, as the project was winding down earlier than expected, I received another call from the agency, Mandy on the line this time. "Scott, we're serving notice," she said. *Not again*, I thought, *not when we're so close to the wedding.*

> But instead of panicking, I made a promise to myself: "I'll find something new. We'll get this wedding, and everything will work out." I did not know how, but I believed it. I started making calls, scouring job listings, until one caught my eye—a contract in Italy with a major drinks company. Why not try it, I thought. And sent in my application along with a few others.

Not long after, the agency called back. "They'd like an interview," the rep said. Shortly after, I was on a video call with Marco from Milan, which went brilliantly, and he referred me to his boss, Jazz. Things were looking up.

Meanwhile, John, the same recruiter who got me the last IT contract, returned from his holiday. When he heard I'd been let go, he was stunned and said he'd find something new for me. Within days, he called back with a solid offer.

Then, the Italian agency reached out. Congratulations, Scott! They want you to start in San Sesto Giovanni." It was enough to make it work.

I called Abi, thrilled with the news. It looks like I'm off to Italy. We celebrated by finally heading out to pick out her engagement ring. Every shop in Chester seemed to have something to try on until she found *the one*. Expensive? Absolutely. But every moment felt worth it.

Then, as fate would have it, John, my original recruiter, rang back with a counteroffer. It was closer to home, more money, and less time away. I struggled with my decision, but my commitment was to the Italian project. Letting John down was hard, but I knew I'd made the right call, even if it meant being away from Abi more than I'd like.

The anxiety about travel was real, but I broke it down into micro-promises.

- **2:00 a.m.** – Get up, shower, and drive to the airport.

- **4:00 a.m.** – Check in and find a strong cup of coffee.

- **6:00 a.m.** – Fly to Bergamo.

- **9:00 a.m.** – Grab a taxi and head straight to the office.

The first day was a whirlwind. Despite being laid back, the Italians had long days. By the time I found food that night, my mixed grill kept me up all night with stomach troubles—hardly the glamorous start I imagined. But the team was welcoming, and the work had a rhythm that kept me focused.

Abi and I talked every night, but by the time we connected, I was so exhausted I could barely keep my eyes open. I think I fell asleep mid-conversation a few times. But each weekend back home, we'd pick up where we left off, shopping for wedding rings and planning every detail.

After Christmas, I returned to Italy, pushing through until March. I took a few weeks off to be back home before the wedding. We had made all arrangements. Abi and I were as ready as we could be, our plans lining up perfectly. All we had left to do was show up and say, "I do."

Then, just as everything seemed secure, my phone buzzed with another call...

CHAPTER TWENTY-SEVEN

AGAINST ALL ODDS

WE NEVER EXPECTED THIS

I couldn't believe what I was hearing. "The airport in Bergamo is closed. They've sent everyone home." Marco's voice was tense. "There's some mysterious virus. People are dying."

"What?" I replied, stunned. "Really? So what do we do?"

"Get everyone set up to work from home. Set up the VPNs, ship out the laptops—we need them operational ASAP." It was like a mission briefing, the urgency crackling through the phone. I'd been staying in the heart of the affected area, so close to being locked down myself. If I hadn't come home early, I'd have been stuck in Italy.

At home, COVID wasn't as widespread, so I shifted focus to work and to the last pieces of wedding planning. The boys and I had a blast getting suited up—Ben was looking sharp, and Tom, well, he could charm a crowd with just a grin. Maisie's dress fitting day came with a tiara, making her look every bit the little princess.

But by the week of the wedding, COVID had spread to the UK. I remember staring at the news, thinking, *Is this actually happening?* My mind raced through all our guests, wondering if it would even be safe. Selfishly, we hoped we'd squeeze the wedding in before the world completely locked down.

A few guests dropped out, especially those in London, not wanting to risk exposure. But the day finally arrived. A sleek limo pulled up to take Ben, Tom, Maisie, and me to the venue. Abi, the beautiful bride, was there early, enjoying a morning of pampering with her friends and Polly.

I felt jittery, a mix of excitement and nerves. As soon as I got to the venue, everyone wanted me for something. "Scott, can you confirm the vows?" "Where are the readings?" The planners had misplaced all the details, so it was lucky I had it all memorised. Seeing our guests waiting, I took a moment to breathe it in.

Then, the music started, and I stood in the aisle, waiting. Abi had joked it might take her a while to walk down, so I braced myself, but every second felt like a year. I could feel everyone looking at me, maybe wondering if she'd even show. Then there she was. Abi stepped into view, radiant, beautiful—she completely took my breath away. My heart did a full somersault.

As she reached my side, I was grinning like a Cheshire cat, unable to contain myself. The vows started, and I lost myself in the moment. At one point, the officiant asked me something, and I went completely blank. I looked around, confused, then blurted, "Sorry, Abi's beauty blindsided me." The entire room erupted in laughter. It ended up being the funniest set of vows I'd ever heard, and we walked down the aisle hand in hand, married at last.

The rest of the day was incredible. We laughed, we danced, and we counted our blessings. The guests who could make it brought such joy, and I felt like the luckiest man alive.

The following morning, we had breakfast with friends, and then the kids returned home. But by that afternoon, the news grew grim—cases were surging, and lockdowns loomed. Italy had already imposed a lockdown, and soon enough, the UK would do the same.

Then my phone rang. It was the boys. "Dad, we can't stay here," Ben said, his voice tense. "Mum is out of control with her drinking,".

"Pack your bags," I told them. "I'll meet you at the train station." With only a few trains still running, they barely made it. I picked them up, disinfected everything, and drove home, just in time for the lockdown to begin.

But the hardest part? I couldn't see Maisie. With Abi as a key worker, we couldn't risk bringing Maisie into the house, and the thought of two months without her felt like torture.

So much for the honeymoon! Now we had a full house: me, Abi, her daughter Polly, and my two boys. None of us had ever lived together before, and there were some adjustments, to say the least. But slowly, we settled into our new lives, finding our rhythm, even if it wasn't the one we'd imagined.

Then, just when I thought we'd found our footing, the phone rang again.

Chapter Twenty-Eight

FULL CIRCLE

Embracing Change, Setbacks, and Building Resilience

The call came in, and Jazz's voice was heavy with regret. Our priorities have shifted, Scott, and I wanted to keep you on, but because of the lockdown, it's not possible.

I stared at the phone, feeling the familiar sting of another job slipping through my fingers. Ben was at the table, revising for his A-levels. He looked up, sensing something was off. "You alright, Dad?"

I tried to mask my frustration. "Just lost the job, son."

Abi walked in, reading the look on my face. "Not again," she said, her eyes filled with sympathy. "Are you okay?"

"I just need some air." I headed outside, grateful for the fresh breeze on my face. With everything already upside down because of the pandemic, this was the last thing we needed. I walked through the country park, thoughts swirling, and found a quiet bench to sit on. Was this just bad luck, or was it something I kept doing wrong?

Right then, I realised a hard truth: I'd been letting life lead me, relying on stability from things I couldn't control. I made a promise to myself: *No more going with the flow. I'm taking charge from here on out.*

Over the next few months, I looked for work but didn't let it consume me. I focused on being present with the kids, spending precious time together. Losing a job was tough, but the silver lining was right there in front of me—moments with my family I wouldn't have had otherwise.

Life, though, has a way of testing resilience. One day, the boys' mum called, pressuring them to come back. When they refused, she showed up at my door. My heart sank as I watched them go. The house felt hollow again, but this time, I knew how to keep going.

And just when things felt settled, another test came knocking—this time in a brown envelope. In the UK, when you see that brown envelope from HMRC, you know it's not a Christmas card. I opened it, heart pounding, and there it was: a demand for nearly £90,000 in taxes from over a decade ago. My mind raced back to that old umbrella company I'd used—they'd been dodgy, and now it was coming back to haunt me.

Abi came home, and I held the letter up. "You won't believe this," I said, showing her the bill.

She glanced at it, her eyes wide for a second, then she burst out laughing. "Honestly, I thought someone had died! It'll be alright, just call them up. It's probably a mistake."

I'd fallen into the same old trap of thinking the world was ending, but Abi's calmness grounded me. I made the call, and thankfully, Abi was right.

They'd made an error—it was still a hefty £16,000, but that was something I could manage.

Life has a way of keeping you on your toes. Each challenge, big or small, builds resilience, a kind of armour against the unpredictable. And over time, you learn you can overcome setbacks, even though they sting. This, too, would pass.

Five years on, life looks vastly different. Mrs Adams the 3rd, as Abi playfully calls herself, and I are still deeply connected, despite the inevitable challenges of a blended family. Our bond isn't just love; it's a partnership forged by laughter, hardship, and growth.

And the kids? They're thriving. Ben graduated with a first in Cyber Security. Just the other day, he called with some news. "Dad, I'm off to Jersey next week...to the zoo!" It turns out he'd be testing security systems at the very place he'd dreamed of working as a kid. Life really has a way of making things come full circle.

Tom is at university in Liverpool, making his own mark on the world, and Polly is in her last year of uni, pushing through challenges that have only strengthened her. Maisie, my youngest, is growing into a vibrant, sassy eleven-year-old, navigating her way through secondary school.

As for Abi, she's shown more resilience than I could ever imagine. Losing her mum was a gut-wrenching loss, but she's pushed forward, reinventing herself with a career in the estate agency business while caring for her dad.

And me? I'm living that promise I made on the park bench. I've built a life around helping others build resilience, showing people it's not just a concept—it's a choice, a practice. Each challenge has led me here, and instead of just surviving, I've learned to thrive.

Looking back, I can see that every setback—the heartbreaks, the job losses, the tax surprises—has shaped who I am. They were lessons, sometimes disguised as disasters. And now, I want to share the frameworks that helped me through it all with you.

So, if you're ready, let's dive into the lessons, the commitments, and the promises that can transform your life, just as they did mine.

Chapter Twenty-Nine

THE POWER OF THOUGHT

Navigating Life's Chaos, Distractions, and Finding Meaning

What I didn't share in earlier chapters is that amidst all the chaos, I was living an incredible life. I'd travelled the world, met people from every continent, coached others, and soaked up experiences that most people only dream about. Life was amazing, not because it was perfect, but because of how I saw it. Now, I won't bore you with pages of what went right; instead, I want to pass on the brief insights I've picked up that might help you navigate your own journey.

> Everything in life starts with a thought.

It's what you do with that thought that shapes you as a person—your choices, how you see yourself, and ultimately, how others see you. Do you remember back at the beginning of this book, I said that most people don't truly know who they are? That's because thoughts are powerful; they can convince you of anything if you dwell on them long enough. Positive or negative, these thoughts shape who you become.

The people I've coached often struggle here. Some thoughts aren't pleasant, right? They challenge your integrity, your self-worth, even your morals, leaving you feeling isolated and sometimes ashamed. But here's the truth: *a thought does not define you.* Acting on that thought is what speaks to your character. We're all human, and sometimes, those knee-jerk reactions are just that—reactions often formed by old patterns, fears, or misconceptions.

Does that mean you're wrong about having those thoughts? Not at all. You're human, and we're wired for survival, carrying instincts that have been with us for thousands of years. We're conditioned through society, education, and culture to think in certain ways, but our initial reactions often come from our raw, unfiltered instincts. Where people struggle is in feeling they need to think like everyone else, conforming to a single "right" way of seeing the world. But the beauty of life is in each of us thinking differently and learning from each other's unique perspectives.

Consider this: if you disagree with someone, do you try to "correct" them immediately, or do you take a moment to listen? In a rush to feel right, we sometimes miss the opportunity to learn. Real growth comes from examining your own thoughts and actions, rather than judging those of others.

Our natural inclination is towards survival. People learn constructs like society, language, and community. From the moment we're born, we're trained to fit within these constructs. And like any learning process, there are hits and misses. Take children, for example: you can shout "HOT!" when they go near the radiator, but chances are, they'll need to touch it at least once to understand why they shouldn't touch it. Experience is the best teacher.

Therefore, you can't really "tell" anyone something. You can advise, but unless they're ready to see it for themselves, the lesson won't stick. Their own experience often sparks that "aha" moment, when someone finally gets it, not what anyone else told them.

Our role in life is to help others, to share our experiences as signposts, not roadmaps. And yet, nothing in school teaches us how to approach life as an adult, especially for balancing work, relationships, and personal growth. We grow up in a bubble, safe in a world where we're rewarded or reprimanded based on rules we know well. Then suddenly, we're adults, faced with paying bills, handling relationships, and figuring out who we are in a world that doesn't care much about our safety net.

The transition is huge. Work becomes the new playground, filled with competition, authority figures, and people who either support or challenge you. But unlike school, where you had the freedom to try things and fail, now you're paid for your contributions and expected to succeed. If you find yourself in a job where you're undervalued, it's worth reassessing. Trying to force yourself to fit where you don't belong is like shoving a round peg into a square hole. Life's too short for that.

And then there's the constant buzz of life around us—the pings and notifications that steal our attention every few seconds. Think back: how many actual emergencies have you had where you needed to be available 24/7? Probably very few. Yet, we're constantly tuned in, afraid of missing out. When we were kids, no one knew where anyone was until they were home. Now, we feel we need to be instantly accessible, and we end up living in a state of constant distraction, missing out on the very life we're trying to stay connected to.

Take a step back and ask yourself: *How many of these thoughts and distractions are actually relevant to me?* For most of us, it's 80% noise and only 20% substance. Imagine if we focused on that 20%—the important stuff right in front of us, rather than the endless stream of other people's lives that pulls us in a million directions.

There's so much more to say about taking control of your thoughts, but I'll stop here for now. In the next chapter, we'll dive deeper into how to break the habit of distraction and live with intention.

Chapter Thirty

QUIETNESS

The Key to Clarity, Sanity, and Maybe Even a Little Less Regret

Quietness is at the core of everything – a calm mind is a mind in control. It's the mind that can actually *think* instead of just reacting. When the world isn't constantly pinging, buzzing, or shouting at you, you get a little mental space to sort things out. You'll start making better decisions, trust me, instead of knee-jerking your way into things that make you wince two days later.

Over the years, I've noticed that the people who seem the most "productive" often have a strange addiction to busyness. They're always on the go, ticking things off, running in circles, and looking like they've just had five espressos. But, more often than not, that constant busyness is just a great disguise for avoidance. I know this because I used to be a master at it. After both of my divorces, I kept my mind racing at warp speed. I thought, if I just kept moving, I could avoid facing the thoughts I really needed to face. Spoiler: it didn't work.

Once I forced myself to slow down, I realised how much I'd been running from myself. Quietness gave me the space to process those thoughts, confront them, and find solutions. It's not about escaping reality; it's about taking a moment to reflect without all the noise. Quietness lets you see that 20% of things that actually matter, instead of the 80% that just makes you anxious.

And yes, the classic answer to this is *meditation*. But let's be honest – how many of us can really see ourselves sitting cross-legged, chanting "om" for 20 minutes without feeling like a right numpty? I thought the same until I realised you don't need to sit on a mountaintop to meditate. It's all about the peace, not the posture. If sitting quietly isn't your style, find a version that works. Walk in the park, sit in the bath, lock yourself in the bathroom for a minute if you have to – whatever gives you that pause.

These quiet moments are golden. When you let things settle, answers have room to appear. Think of how often you've snapped at someone, rushed a response, or made a choice only to think, *What was I doing?* Later on. Your mind was so cluttered, you couldn't see straight. Quiet time allows you to pause, gather your thoughts, and respond with purpose. And remember, you don't always have to respond straight away – if you need time to think, just say it. It's far better than rushing and regretting.

Of course, there are moments in life when decisions are instant, and there's no time for quiet. But if you train your mind to enjoy those calm, reflective moments, even quick decisions will come more naturally. A quiet mind is like a muscle – the more you use it, the stronger it gets.

And if you're wondering, yes, formal meditation is worth a shot, but if it isn't for you, fair enough. Just find your own version of quiet and commit to it. This pause isn't just for clarity; it's for your sanity, resilience, and overall happiness. Quietness, in any form, is what will keep you grounded, keep you calm, and keep you from snapping at the wrong people when they don't deserve it – which, let's face it, is most of the time.

Chapter Thirty-One

LISTENING

The Superpower We All Overlook

Listening is one of life's greatest gifts. I'm not kidding – it's probably the most underrated superpower you can develop. For years, I thought I was an expert in it, even though I jumped in before anyone finished talking. I still want to interrupt – a habit that's hard to kick even at 52. But we're always learning, and I'm still working on refining the art of *actually* listening.

If you don't truly listen, you're only ever going to hear half the story. The other half? That's left to your own imagination, and we all know how that usually plays out. So let's dig into why listening well is so important and how it can genuinely change your perspective on life.

When I was young, I loved talking to my grandparents, hearing their stories. Their lives were so different – baths in metal tubs, food rations, kids shipped off to the countryside for safety. Then there were the men who signed up for war at sixteen, faced bombs, saw friends fall in battle – and came home to a world that expected them to get on with it, pub and pint in hand. Back then, they didn't acknowledge anxiety and PTSD; Listening to their stories showed me how lucky I was to grow up in a time of peace and opportunity. It was those conversations that taught me the importance of empathy and respect for the older generation, who faced far more than I ever would.

Then there was Mark, my mentor, back in my estate agent days. He'd always say, *"Let the buyer do the talking; they'll tell you what they need."* It sounds simple, but it's a game-changer. I can't tell you how many times I've watched people barrel through a conversation without letting the other person get to the point. All it takes is giving them that space, and they'll reveal everything you need to know. This principle applies in all areas of life, not just sales. It's like practising a kind of mental martial art, holding back until they finish, so you don't miss the important bit.

Listening in Relationships: The Glue that Holds Things Together

If you're in a relationship, listening is non-negotiable. You don't have to agree with every word, but if they're talking, you owe it to them to listen. I see it all the time in my coaching work: one partner stops feeling heard, and suddenly communication grinds to a halt. In relationships, lack of listening can start as a crack and end up as a canyon.

With kids, it's the same story, but with a twist. They're learning the ropes, testing limits, and finding their way in the world. When they're frustrated, it's rare that they are aware of what they're actually doing. It's often about something deeper. Instead of shouting, try this: *"Why do you feel this way? What do you think will help?"* You'll get far better results, and the communication stays open rather than shutting down and shouting at them.

One of the biggest challenges I see is parents who assume the kid is the problem without looking at their own reactions. It's understandable – kids can push every button you have. But sometimes, if you take a beat and really listen, you'll notice it's your reaction that needs adjusting. Trust me, kids get enough discipline from life as it is; home should be where they're heard and understood.

Expanding Your World through Listening

Listening isn't just for the people you know – it's for everyone you meet. Talking to people from different backgrounds, cultures, and life experiences is like picking up a free encyclopaedia. You get insights and perspectives that can completely transform how you view the world. There's so much out there that school never taught us, and listening to others is your way to keep learning.

Here's the thing: **Knowledge is power.** But it's not just about what you know; it's about understanding what others know. Whether it's a new perspective on life, an insight into a different culture, or even just a new way of doing things, listening is your gateway to a richer, more nuanced understanding of the world.

So, next time you're with someone, put the phone down. Be present, listen, and let them finish their story. You'll be surprised by how much you learn - and how much your relationships, both personal and professional, start to improve when you are present, listen, and let them finish their story.

CHAPTER THIRTY-TWO

LETTING GO OF BLAME

THE GIFT OF MOVING FORWARD

Blame can be a hefty burden, and for years, I carried it like an unwanted rucksack, weighing down every step. I blamed my mum for leaving my dad, turning every issue in my life back to that point, hurling my pain at her like it was a cure. I was relentless, convinced that she needed to understand how her choice had "wrecked" everything for me. But all the while, she was carrying her own hurt. She'd made the hardest decision of her life, thinking I'd go with her, that I'd want to be by her side.

But I couldn't leave my dad. And maybe that's where the real resentment lay – it was my choice, and I felt trapped in it. I held onto that resentment for years, letting it fester like an open wound. And then, during my first divorce, I was at my mum's house, nursing a glass (or three) of wine, dredging up the same old speech, my tired excuses. And then, in a tearful voice, she said, *"Scott, please, I can't take this anymore."*

In that moment, I saw it for what it was – a relentless cycle of blaming her, blaming everyone but myself. My marriage was falling apart, and there I was, sitting in her kitchen with all the irony in the world. How would I feel if my own kids came to me one day, blaming me for everything? Hypocrisy never tasted so bitter. From that moment, I let it go. She was right; it wasn't her fault, and my constant blame would not change a thing. And frankly, she didn't deserve it.

> That experience taught me more than I expected. I realised I'd also been holding a grudge against my dad for not wanting me to leave the army. I'd spun that story in my head so long it had become my truth. Finally, I went to him, and what did I find out? A massive misunderstanding. Years of bitterness, and it was all built on something that wasn't even true.

That realisation was freeing. Now, my relationship with my mum and dad is stronger than ever. I'm grateful I let go when I did. Every week, I take my dad out to play pool – making up for lost time. Blame had kept us apart, but understanding brought us back together.

Letting Go in Relationships: Sarah and Jenny's Lessons

In the same way, I carried a truckload of resentment toward Sarah. Why couldn't she see the good in what we had? Why wasn't what I gave her enough? But then I looked at my boys. I realised that without everything we'd gone through, they wouldn't be here, wouldn't be in my life the way they are now. That thought alone helped me release my anger toward her. Sarah's choices were hers to make, her happiness her own to pursue. My job was to move forward, not get bogged down by her choices.

Then came Jenny. When she ended our marriage, I was gutted. She knew what I'd gone through in my first divorce – how could she end it all so abruptly? But with time, I saw she was right. When I moved on from the hurt and examined things objectively, it became clear that we had never truly been compatible. It took courage for her to leave, to stay firm even when she knew it would be easier to give in. Jenny didn't talk about it because she knew deep down it wouldn't work, and she didn't want to be talked out of it. I came to respect that bravery.

Hindsight is a gift, isn't it? Looking back from a better place in life, it's clear that everything was setting me up for something greater. All those heartbreaks? They were getting me ready to treat Mrs Adams the 3rd the right way, to truly appreciate and cherish what I have with her now.

The Freedom in Forgiving

Letting go of blame isn't about excusing others; it's about freeing yourself. Blame holds you back, ties you to the past, and clouds your future. The best thing you can do is forgive – not for them, but for yourself. Learn the lesson and let go, because those old stories don't define who you're becoming.

So, drop the blame. Forgive the past, embrace the future, and take those lessons forward. Life is much lighter without the weight.

CHAPTER THIRTY-THREE

THE POWER OF HONESTY

WITH OTHERS AND YOURSELF

Honesty really is a game-changer—and I'm not just talking about being straight with yourself. It's about extending that honesty to everyone in your life. We've talked about how 80% of the thoughts running through your mind are just noise, pointless chatter. But that other 20%? That's the stuff that matters, and it's where honesty becomes essential.

You can't expect someone to understand how you feel if you haven't actually told them. Have you ever simmered over something, replaying every detail in your mind, getting worked up while they're totally oblivious to it? It's easy to convince ourselves that people "should just know," but here's the truth—most people can't read minds. When we don't speak up, we set ourselves up to be disappointed and resentful. And I'll be honest: I've been there myself.

In the past, I'd get wound up, convinced someone was intentionally doing things just to get on my nerves. But then I'd realise they hadn't a clue it even bothered me. Many of my coaching clients share this pattern. They're frustrated with their partners, friends, family members, convinced that "they should know" what's wrong. But without honesty, it's just a loop of unspoken grievances. You think you're avoiding conflict, but in reality, you're creating tension. And people always sense that tension, even if it's not voiced.

Being honest doesn't mean spilling everything out in one emotional outburst just because you can't hold it in anymore. It's about attempting to talk openly about what's really on your mind. We often make things worse by pre-judging how the conversation will go, thinking there's no point because we've already decided the outcome. But by doing this, we rob ourselves—and the other person—of the chance for genuine connection and understanding.

Honesty Isn't Always Comfortable, But It's Essential

Facing an issue head-on is rarely easy. There's a discomfort to it, sure. Maybe you worry about hurting them, or you just don't want to deal with the awkwardness. But here's the thing—if you're not willing to talk about it, you lose the right to judge them for not knowing. Expecting someone to figure out what's wrong through silence is like expecting a brick wall to respond. Without honest communication, they'll never have the chance to make things right.

This also comes down to being honest with yourself. If you've done something you regret, or let yourself down, don't hide behind excuses or pride. Acknowledge it, own it, and, if needed, make it right. Self-honesty is the foundation for growth. None of us is perfect, and the sooner we admit when we're wrong, the sooner we can make genuine progress.

Be Real with Yourself – No Excuses

Honesty doesn't just apply to our relationships with others. If there's something in your life that's not right—whether it's your health, your career, or a habit you're trying to break—being honest with yourself is the first step. Complaining won't get you anywhere if you're not prepared to take action. Take weight loss, for instance. There's no sense looking in the mirror, calling yourself out, and then doing nothing about it. If you're not ready to change, own it and be proud of where you are. Don't let harsh self-talk drag you down if you're not genuinely motivated to make a change.

If it is something you want to change, then be honest about what it'll take. Genuine honesty means accepting where you are without judgement but being clear-eyed about where you want to be. This applies to the little things too, like feeling uncomfortable speaking up in certain situations. If you're holding back on expressing yourself, you've got to look at why and tackle it. Avoiding these conversations just reinforces that discomfort, and it prevents any actual change.

Find Your Voice, Create Change

If you make it a habit to speak up, especially in situations that make you uncomfortable, you'll see a shift. Avoiding hard conversations doesn't protect you; it only keeps you stuck in a loop of intrusive thoughts and missed opportunities. Taking small steps to express yourself more openly can make all the difference. Life becomes simpler when you get comfortable discussing what's on your mind.

So here's the bottom line: honesty is a foundation. It's how you keep things real with others and, more importantly, with yourself. It's not just about telling the truth but about living it—speaking up, taking accountability, and making decisions that truly align with who you are.

The journey might be uncomfortable at first, but as you get better at it, life has a way of opening up in ways you never expected. So start small, have those honest conversations, and watch how much lighter life becomes when you're true to yourself.

Chapter Thirty-Four

Looking After Yourself

The Lesson That Took Me Years to Learn

This one's taken me ages to figure out, and even now, I still trip up sometimes. I was that person who always put everyone else first. Need help? I was there. Something needed doing? Drop everything; Scott's on it. And for a while, it seemed like the right thing – like the noble thing, even.

But then it caught up with me. Somewhere along the line, I lost myself in it all. The gym sessions I loved? Gone. The quiet time I needed to clear my head? Sacrificed. Nights out with friends? Barely a memory. My life had become this merry-go-round of meeting everyone else's needs, and I wasn't even on my list.

Eventually, resentment crept in. I was there for everyone, yet I started feeling bitter. "Why doesn't anyone look out for me?" I thought. But here's the thing yet again – it wasn't them; it was me. I'd abandoned myself in the name of "helping" and "supporting." I thought it was their fault that I wasn't living the life I wanted, but in reality, I'd handed them the reins.

And it wasn't just family. In relationships, this habit showed up like clockwork. I'd plan to do something for myself, and suddenly, I'd get the "Do you really need to go?" or the "Wouldn't you rather stay in?" And rather than being honest about what I needed, I'd fold every time. In my mind, I was doing it for them, but in reality, I was just avoiding an honest conversation – and that helped no one.

I'd become so wrapped up in the idea of "us" that I'd forgotten the "me" part. We'd build these routines where it was just us all the time, and when life started demanding more, they felt neglected, and I felt trapped. All because I hadn't set the right boundaries from the start.

So, who was to blame? Me. It wasn't their fault; it was mine. I'd chosen to stay silent, to say "yes" when I wanted to say "no," to skip things I enjoyed for the sake of "keeping the peace." I never explained that it wasn't about not wanting to be with them – I just had other needs, too.

The Importance of Taking Your Own Time

Looking after yourself is essential. You need that time, those activities, those moments that are just yours. Take it from someone who's been around the block on this one: you can't pour from an empty cup. It's like clocking into a job – you need your own "clock-in" time for your well-being.

It's still a challenge for me. I've learned that if you're going to give, do it freely and expect nothing in return. And, most importantly, don't blame others for your choices. If you're always the one putting yourself last, that's on you.

So, take that time. Do what makes you happy, and then show up as a better, more balanced version of yourself in your relationships. It's one of the most worthwhile lessons I've learned, and I'm still getting better at it every day.

Chapter Thirty-Five

FEAR

That Devil on Your Shoulder

Fear is that little devil whispering in your ear, telling you, "You can't do it." It shows up in different ways and, if you've followed my story, you'll know I took on fear headfirst from a young age, using a simple promise. And that promise worked. Since then, I haven't been afraid to face anything. The reason? Because the cost of giving in to fear is massive – it means missing out on moments and experiences that could shape your life in ways you never imagined.

Fear mostly lives in that 80% of thoughts that swirl around in our heads. The real problem, the bit that actually needs addressing, sits in the 20% that you can deal with. The mind is complex, but it's also programmable. If you repeatedly tell yourself you "can't," your mind will believe it. On the flip side, tell yourself you *can*, and your mind will simply get on with it.

I learned this lesson the hard way with my driving anxiety. I'd been driving perfectly well for years. But after one panic attack on a dual carriageway where I couldn't pull over, fear dug its claws in. The mere thought of getting behind the wheel was enough to make me sweat, even though I wasn't anywhere near a car. The problem wasn't driving – it was the story I'd created around it.

Consider this: whenever my mind was on something else, I would get in the car, and everything would be fine. But the minute I jumped in while thinking about every "what if" imaginable, that's when it fell apart. My story had become my reality. I had to rewrite that story. I said to myself, "I'm a skilled driver. I adore this sense of freedom. It's a lovely day for a drive." It flipped my story entirely.

It's easy to get trapped in a narrative of fear, especially when it's just a bad habit we've unknowingly built. Fear is a powerful thing, and it stops plenty of people from living fully. When I work with my coaching clients, we often have to unpack these stories and build a new framework for their confidence. It's totally possible if you're willing to shift your mindset.

Now, I've got a bit of a system: if a thought pops into my head, I ask myself, "Would I be happy if this came true?" If the answer is no, I mentally toss it into what I like to call the "bucket of useless thoughts" and move on. This helps me cut through the noise, take action, and stay focused.

When I started the job in Italy, I didn't let fear take control. I broke the journey down into steps, wrote the story in my mind with each move, and handled it one bit at a time until I arrived without a hitch. No panic, just progress.

So if you're struggling with fear, take some quiet time to make yourself a promise. Rewrite the story in your mind. Create a better narrative, one where fear takes a back seat, and you're in the driver's seat, headed exactly where you want to go.

Chapter Thirty-Six

ACCOUNTABILITY
The Thing Everyone Dislikes

Accountability is at the heart of who we are—how we act, what we say, and ultimately, what we build with our lives. It's about taking responsibility for our choices, owning up to our actions, and being honest, not just with others, but with ourselves. From a young age, I learned this lesson, thanks to my brother, who would blame me for everything. By quickly realising that telling the truth allowed my mum to spot his lies. I didn't love being "the honest one" all the time, but I saw early on how owning up could benefit me. Putting it all on the table lifted the weight of "what if someone finds out" off my shoulders. I found that people actually trusted me more and wanted to help because I'd been honest.

From that point on, I tried to apply this same honesty across my life. I realised that lying, or even skirting around the truth, only creates layers of confusion—layers that eventually trap you in your own fiction. You can even start believing your own storylines. So, I decided on a simpler approach: act with kindness, listen, and say what I believe is right. If I'm wrong, I apologise and adjust. But once I've done my part, if a situation spirals out of control, it's no longer on me—I've done what I can. This approach to accountability brings an enormous sense of relief and clarity.

This philosophy became a pillar of my life, especially in my marriages. After each one ended, I made a promise to change so I wouldn't end up in the same position again. I wanted to grow, to become a better partner and, more than anything, to break the cycle. Ironically, it took three marriages to really grasp the importance of accountability. But each one taught me something. Looking back, I can see my part in the problems of those first two marriages, though I couldn't see it clearly. It's easy to miss when you're in the thick of it. Hindsight, though, was a game-changer for me. Owning up to my role in things wasn't just humbling; it was empowering. When you see the impact of your own actions, you gain the power to make better choices next time.

This self-accountability is something I see a lot with my coaching clients, too. Many people are stuck in the blame game, convinced that they have just had "bad partners" or have been surrounded by "narcissists." I always remind them we're viewed differently by each person in our lives—our parents, friends, partners. They each interact with us based on their understanding of who we are, which is shaped by our actions.

When you embrace accountability, you open yourself up to change. You take charge of your part in things, rather than just reacting to what others do. Even if others don't change, that you've done everything in your power frees you from the situation. Accountability is the ultimate freedom, giving you the clarity and confidence to walk away from a situation, knowing you've done all you can. And that's enough.

CHAPTER THIRTY-SEVEN

HABITS

6 WEEKS TO FORM - 1 DAY TO BREAK

Habits shape our lives, for better or worse. They're the backbone of our daily actions and the reason most people struggle to follow through on promises, even ones they're deeply committed to. Building a habit takes more than just the will to do something; it requires structure and a routine. And it doesn't have to be the same routine every day, but there has to be *some* kind of plan to keep you on course. Without direction, no amount of promises can keep you moving forward.

Take losing weight. If it were easy, everyone would do it. But people often set themselves up with impossible routines and expectations, don't stick with them long enough to see results, and then quit. For me, it usually takes about six weeks for a new habit to feel natural. And yes, there are slip-ups.

When Abi and I first moved in together, we wanted to start off on the right foot, so we openly shared our pet peeves. For Abi, it was simple: "Put the toilet seat down and make sure the tap's facing forward." Minor details, right? But I wanted to respect her requests, so I made a conscious effort every day to do just those things. Now, it's a reflex—I even do it in public restrooms! It's proof that a simple routine, repeated consistently, turns into a habit.

Then there's the gym. I'm up at 5:30 a.m., and people think I'm mad. But once it became a habit, I stopped seeing it as "getting up early" or "missing sleep." Instead, it's "great, another day to crush it and get the gym in before life gets busy." Of course, in the beginning, it wasn't easy. But I got past that initial resistance by treating each morning as a micro-commitment. No snoozing, no excuses—just getting up and going.

The trick to forming habits? Make a conscious decision to start and combine it with a micro-promise about how you'll follow through. Don't dive in too deep; small steps create sustainable routines. When I first started, I just went on walks in the hills, because jumping straight into high-intensity workouts would've had me quitting in no time. Begin with something manageable, like meditating after you brush your teeth, and keep stacking little habits until they become effortless parts of your day.

Why do some habits stick so easily while others fall apart? Often, it's because we don't see them as essential. If showing up to a 6 a.m. workout was the only way to keep your job. You'd be there, no questions asked. Apply that level of commitment to personal promises. Remind yourself that not following through has consequences. Without accountability, we cut corners if we think we can get away with it.

So, treat your new habits as non-negotiable. Start small, build momentum, and watch yourself grow. Once you see the results, you'll naturally want to keep going.

CHAPTER THIRTY-EIGHT

THE COURAGE TO SPEAK

BUILDING HONEST CONNECTIONS IN LIFE

You know, it doesn't matter who you're talking to – partner, kids, workmates – if you're not sharing what's really on your mind, you're just talking at each other. For years, I avoided it. I'd bury myself in my own assumptions, convincing myself people didn't get me. Truth was, they probably would've understood... if I'd just been honest.

We've all been there, right? Those moments where you avoid saying what you need to because you're afraid of the answer or can't seem to find the courage. It's natural, but here's the thing – speaking up about hard stuff is a skill. And like any skill, you can get better at it.

But don't get me wrong; it's not about blurting out the first thing that comes to mind. It's about slowing down, really gathering what you want to say, and then getting it all out without holding back. Most of the time, the frustration kicks in because the other person interrupts, thinking they need to fix it before you've even finished. And let's be honest – that's infuriating. But that's where you've got to stick to your guns. Keep going until you've put all your thoughts on the table.

If you walk away feeling unheard or frustrated, it's on you to keep that conversation going until it's done right. They deserve a chance to respond to the real you – not some half-baked version because you're afraid of their reaction.

A perfect example? Ben, my youngest. He stayed with me over the holidays. I thought I was supporting him, being the dad I should, but there was this constant tension, this friction I couldn't put my finger on. No matter what I tried – a walk, a pint, or just a chat – he was snapping at me, and I couldn't figure out why.

Then, three months later, it all came out. Turns out, Ben had failed his first year at uni and hadn't told me because he thought I'd lose it. And yeah, when he finally told me... I lost it. But not because he failed – I got that part, totally understood. It was the fact he'd bottled it up, decided my reaction without even giving me the chance to prove him wrong.

So I said, "Ben, mate, why didn't you just tell me?"

He goes, "Dad, I knew you'd blow your fuse. You were always on about working hard, and I just... couldn't tell you."

After the dust settled, I called him back. I knew I'd overreacted. I told him, "Look, I'm sorry for the way I reacted. Let's figure out a plan together."

We sat down, mapped out his next steps, and he ended up switching to a new degree in the same city, happier and surrounded by his mates again. It all worked out, but it reminded me just how important it is to speak up, especially when we assume we know how others will react.

So, don't hold on to things and judge how someone's going to respond before you even give them a chance. Conversations can be tough, but they're worth it. You'll get better with practice, and soon enough, it'll become a habit – a good one, at that. Trust me, being honest with others and with yourself can change your entire perspective.

CHAPTER THIRTY-NINE

RELENTLESS PURSUIT

THE POWER OF NOT GIVING UP

When I proposed to Abi, people asked me, *Why on Earth would you want to get married again?* After two marriages that didn't work out, why not just settle, let go of the dream, play it safe? But here's the thing: I don't believe in defeat. I would not let two broken marriages define my life, my happiness, or the family I'd always imagined. The vision of a loving, supportive family was mine to shape, and I would let no one or anything take that away.

The idea of "third time lucky" didn't even matter—it wasn't about luck. It was about not letting past experiences dictate the rest of my life. We can't judge our entire journey by one or two wrong turns. We can't quit just because the road feels endless or because rejection feels like it's too much to bear. Often, we're far closer to the finish line than we realise; most people give up just a step or two before success. And when we stop, what happens? We're right back where we started, facing the same frustrations and wondering why.

Life isn't meant to be easy—we all face rejection, struggles, and setbacks. But look closely at those who've achieved their dreams. You might think, *It's easy for them*, but you haven't seen the sacrifices, the self-reflection, and the battles they've endured to get there. Behind every win is resilience, patience, and relentless persistence.

> If you're on the verge of giving up, remember this: you might be a single day away from everything you've worked for. Don't let that slip through your fingers. Taking a pause to catch your breath is fine, but don't let it turn into giving up.

In the future, you may look back and wish you'd taken that one more step. The only time it's right to stop is when you truly know that the road has ended—when it's beyond your control. And even then, don't give up on yourself; just pivot, redirect that drive, and keep moving forward, testing your abilities and breaking new ground.

Pushing yourself to the limits may lead to surprising yourself at how far you can go. Climb your own mountains, endure the pain, and when you finally reach that peak, you'll look out, see the vastness of what you've accomplished, and know it was worth every moment.

CHAPTER FORTY

PATIENCE

IS IT REALLY A VIRTUE

They say patience is a virtue, right? But what does that mean in real life when your neck-deep in deadlines, everyone's after you, and your phone's pinging every five seconds? It's like a pressure cooker, and all you want is an answer, a solution, anything to clear some space in your head and lighten the load. I've been there, and believe me, I was once the most impatient person you could imagine. I wanted to sort everything out, handle everything, and get everything done—because to me, being in control meant having things handled. I thought that if I could just keep all the plates spinning, I'd have everything I needed.

But life doesn't work like that, and chasing constant control led to more frustration than success. Sure, some of my quick decisions worked out, but looking back, I realise some things would've been better if I'd just stepped back. Over time, I learned that if something doesn't need an immediate solution; you don't have to react straight away. Most things, unless they're emergencies, will wait.

Think about it. You've probably heard people say their best ideas come when they're in the shower, out walking, or just sitting quietly. Why? Because when you stop reacting and let your mind settle, it can actually think. I can't count the number of times I acted in haste, only to find I'd missed a much better solution that came to me later.

Next time something big lands on your plate, resist the urge to respond immediately. Instead, make a note of it and let it simmer. Go about your day, give it some background thought, consider the options. This approach has saved me countless times, helping me see solutions I'd have missed in a rush. It allows your mind to open up to possibilities instead of latching onto the first available answer.

We're conditioned to think that everything needs to be done now. It doesn't. Sometimes, you'll find that letting it sit actually makes the problem seem smaller, more manageable. I've noticed that if something doesn't feel clear, there's probably a reason for it, and forcing an answer rarely makes things better. Instead, come back to it later, maybe tomorrow. It's amazing how a fresh mind can turn a mountain into a molehill.

You've heard the saying, "No news is good news." But how often do we actually sit comfortably with that idea? We jump to conclusions, assuming the worst. This, too, is where patience comes in. Learn to direct your mind elsewhere, especially when you have no control over the outcome.

If you find yourself stressed out by making decisions or waiting for answers, take a step back. Give it time. You'll be amazed at how often you find the right answer when you stop chasing it.

Chapter Forty-One

FINDING BALANCE

Creating Harmony in Life's Demands

One of life's most challenging pursuits is balance. My friend's grand-mother once told me, *"Life will always be a compromise,"* and while I paid little attention, that phrase has echoed back to me repeatedly. When I reflect, I see so many moments where I was off balance. You might feel this too, or maybe you've found your stride. If you have, then honestly, hats off to you – achieving balance is no small feat.

In my early years, I was driven, hungry for success, and nothing would stand in my way. I travelled endlessly for work, often coming home ex-hausted, which took its toll on my relationships. Being too drained pre-vented me from being fully present for my kids. Being too focused on my career hindered me from nurturing my marriage, and being too busy kept me from prioritising the things I loved. I didn't see it then, but striving for success without maintaining balance was costing me more than I realised.

Balancing health, wealth, and relationships equally is the aim, because what's the point of success if you're constantly at odds with your family? What good is robust health if you have no one to enjoy it with? And how fulfilling can a relationship be if financial or health issues constantly loom? True balance is about aligning all aspects of life, so each supports the other.

Creating balance starts with honest conversations. Be upfront about your goals with those around you, but equally, consider their needs. Set boundaries so that everyone knows when you need time for work, when family takes precedence, and when you need a bit of time for yourself. This isn't about being rigid; it's about setting a rhythm that brings peace to all parties involved.

And let's be real – it's no secret why they say money doesn't always equal happiness. Financial success can come with intense responsibilities and stress, often at the expense of health and relationships. Balance is about knowing when to step back from work to focus on family or health, or to say no to that extra commitment. It's about understanding that just as you might need your own time, others need quality time with you too – the kind where you're fully present, not half-distracted or glued to a screen.

It's okay to be open about what you can give or can't give and to decline where needed respectfully. Saying "no" doesn't mean neglecting responsibilities; it means valuing balance in your life. And if you're finding life pulling you in too many directions, take a step back. Look at where you're giving too much, and see if you can shift things. Balance isn't about perfection – it's about adjusting and realigning until you find a pace that lets you give, enjoy, and live without feeling stretched too thin.

Chapter Forty-Two

THE POWER OF A PROMISE

Changing Your Life One Promise At A Time

Picture a life where you craft a vision for yourself and align every choice, every action with it. A life where you're not simply going through the motions, but actively creating a path towards something truly meaningful. This is the power of a promise—a commitment that grounds you, shapes your journey, and keeps you moving forward, even on the hardest days.

When you make a promise to yourself, you're doing more than setting a goal. You're committing to a principle that represents who you are and what you stand for. A promise becomes an unshakable guide, pushing you to act even when motivation is nowhere in sight. It's a declaration that what you want matters enough to tackle the obstacles and discomfort that lie ahead.

Think about it: how often have you held back from something meaningful because of doubt or fear? How often have you let setbacks dictate your journey, felt weighed down by self-doubt, or given up on a goal because it felt too big? This is where the power of a promise truly shines. A promise isn't just about achieving something; it's about cultivating re-silience, building habits that serve you, and moving with purpose.

Why a Promise is Transformational

As we've discussed, blame, self-worth, resilience, and self-doubt are common struggles. By focusing on the areas you need most—whether it's building confidence, developing better habits, or tackling self-doubt—your promises will help you move past what's held you back. Imagine committing to a promise to improve in an area you've struggled with for years. In six weeks, you'll look back and realise how far you've come, how much more confident you feel, and how much stronger you are for sticking with it.

A promise is a bold statement. It says *I can overcome this,* and even more importantly, *I will.* This isn't about creating massive changes overnight; it's about making intentional, achievable commitments that, overtime, build the foundation of the life you want. And when you look back, you'll find a new level of self-belief and pride that you followed through. This is where true transformation begins.

Crafting Your Promise: A Practical Guide

To make your promise stick, it needs to be deeply personal and meaningful. Here's how to create promises that become the backbone of your journey:

1. **Start with Your Core Values** Ask yourself: *What do I stand for? What's most important to me?* Who do i want to be seen as? Identifying your core values is essential because promises anchored in your values have a way of sticking—they're not negotiable. Whether it's family, health, growth, or resilience, your values give your promises substance.

2. **Identify Areas You Want to Strengthen** Think about where you need growth most. Maybe it's overcoming self-doubt, becoming more disciplined, or learning to forgive yourself. These promises are the ones that matter because they address areas that hold you back. Write one or two key areas where you know a commitment will make a difference.

3. **Create a Bold but Achievable Promise** The best promises are clear and specific. Rather than saying, *"I want to be more confident,"* say, *"I promise to challenge my self-doubt by speaking up at least once in every meeting."* Specific promises keep you grounded and give you something to measure against.

4. **Map Your Promises to Your Vision** Picture your life in six months or a year if you stick to these promises. Visualise the results: a healthier you, a more present parent, or a stronger leader. Mapping your promises to this long-term vision makes them more than just daily tasks; they're stepping stones towards something bigger.

Building Momentum: How to Make Your Promises Stick

Promises are only as strong as your follow-through. Let's make sure you stay on track with these practical steps:

1. **Micro-Promises: The Key to Building Habits** Starting with a big promise can feel overwhelming, so break it down. Instead of promising to "get fit," make a micro-promise like *"I'll walk for 15 minutes each day."* Small, consistent actions are the foundation of lasting habits and will gradually build your confidence.

2. **Accountability: Don't Keep it to Yourself** Share your promises with someone you trust. This could be a friend, partner, or mentor. Or even write them down and place them somewhere visible. Being accountable makes promises feel real, like a binding contract with yourself.

3. **Regular Reflection: Keep Track of Your Progress** Set aside time each week to reflect on your progress. Ask yourself, *Did I honour my promise? How can I improve?* Regular check-ins help you stay committed and give you a chance to adjust if necessary.

4. **Celebrate Your Wins** Acknowledge every step forward, no matter how small. Celebrate your progress, whether it's keeping a promise for a week or seeing a shift in how you feel. Celebrating reinforces the behaviour, making it easier to keep going. Give yourself a massive pat on the back or a high five in the mirror.

5. **Forgive, Don't Quit** If you slip up, forgive yourself quickly. The path isn't perfect, but it's about persistence. When you stumble, remind yourself of why you started, refocus, and keep moving

forward. One misstep doesn't undo your progress.

Your Promise, Your Legacy

Imagine looking back on your life and seeing a path shaped by promises kept. Promises aren't just about achieving goals; they're about building a life that reflects who you truly are. And, as you honour your promises, you're creating a legacy—a story of resilience, purpose, and integrity.

This is your invitation to start now. What's one promise you can make today? One commitment that, if kept, will shape the rest of your life. Write it down, own it, and let it be the start of a journey you'll look back on with pride.

Action Challenge: Start with One Promise Today

Choose one promise that aligns with who you want to become. Keep it small, focused,and personal. Start with a simple daily action, like *"I promise to spend 10minutes each day reading for my personal growth,"* or *"I promise to reach out to one friend a week."* Small steps, when repeated, create powerful habits.

Let Your Promises Lead You Forward

Each promise is a building block in the life you're crafting, a commitment to not just getting by, but to living fully. These promises don't just change your habits; they reshape how you see yourself. Embrace them. Use them to propel yourself forward. And remember, you're not just making promises—you're creating the person you'll become.

Chapter Forty-Three

STAYING COMMITTED TO YOUR SELF-PROMISES

Creating the Life You Want

As you near the final chapter of this book, remember—this isn't the end of your journey. In fact, it's just the beginning. Throughout these chapters, we've dived deep into the power of self-promises, resilience, balance, accountability, and so much more. Now, it's time to bring it all together and reflect on how you can continue staying committed to the promises you've made to yourself as you move forward.

This chapter serves as your closing reflection and a reminder that the life you want is within reach—as long as you stay true to those promises.

My Journey with Self-Promises

The hardest promise I made to myself was to not sink into negativity and fear of the future. After a couple of breakdowns, I was standing on the edge, and the voices in my head kept telling me what a failure I was. It became hard to concentrate, hard to move forward, and impossible to be present in the moment. My thoughts poisoned me, crippling me for months.

But I made a promise to myself: I wouldn't stay down. That was my anchor. It wasn't about flipping a switch; it was about battling day by day to get back to a better space. I held onto that promise, and it got me through. It's the same promise I keep today when life throws a spanner at me—it's a commitment to myself, a reminder that I'll keep going no matter how tough it gets.

What's the hardest promise you've made to yourself? How did keeping it transform your life, and how did it anchor you during difficult times?

The Power of Realigning Your Vision

One thing I've learned over time is to be careful when making promises. They aren't just throw away commitments—they're the foundation of how you're building your life. Sometimes, life happens, and you drop the ball. It's inevitable. What matters is what you do next. Do you quit? Or do you realign your vision, adjust your approach, and try again?

I've failed at promises before—personally and professionally. But I learned that failure doesn't mean the promise wasn't valid. It just means you need to tweak your path. Stay committed to the bigger vision, even if the road isn't smooth. Realign your goals, adjust your expectations, and keep pushing forward.

Reflect on a time when you broke a self-promise. Write about how you felt, what you learned, and how you realigned your vision to keep moving forward.

Resilience: Your Lifeline Through the Storm

I've faced countless struggles, and at this point in my life, resilience feels like second nature. Life throws its punches, and with each experience, you build a history that reminds you—you'll get through it. It's the fear of the unknown that shakes us, not the challenges we've already faced. My scond divorce was easier than my first, because I built resilience and knew what to expect the second time round.

Resilience, for me, is about holding onto the rails when the path feels unsteady, but trusting that I can make it through to the other side. My values have evolved over the years, and now, more than ever, I realise that peace and inner strength are everything. You outgrow toxic people, learn to forgive for your own peace of mind, and understand that life will always have its difficulties. But if you're still standing, you've got a shot at making things better.

What's one challenge that tested your resilience? How did you dig deep and find the strength to push through? What has that experience taught you about your ability to bounce back?

CHAPTER FORTY-FOUR

LOOKING AHEAD

THE JOURNEY CONTINUES

As you move forward, remember that your self-promise journey is ongoing. The life you want is there for the taking, but it requires continued commitment, reflection, and action. You've built a sound foundation through this book, and now it's about putting those lessons into practice every day.

Think of your self-promises as a map. Sometimes the path will be clear, and other times it'll be rocky and filled with unexpected detours. But as long as you stay true to your promises, you'll always find your way. That's the key—you trust that you've got what it takes, and when things get tough, resilience will see you through.

Reflect on the self-promises you've made throughout your journey. How much headway have you made? What challenges have you overcome? What new promises will you make moving forward?

Revisiting Key Lessons

Before we close this chapter, let's recap some of the key lessons you've learned throughout this book. These are your guiding principles as you continue your self-promise journey:

The Power of Self-Promises: Every promise you make is a step toward the life you want to create. Staying committed builds confidence, resilience, and a deep sense of purpose.

Resilience and adaptability: Life throws spanners. It's not about avoiding setbacks; it's about bouncing back and finding new ways forward.

Balance and Fulfilment: Achieving balance across all areas of life ensures long-term fulfilment. Your promises must support your personal growth, relationships, and well-being.

Gratitude and Reflection: Regular reflection keeps you grounded. Celebrating your wins and reflecting on your progress reminds you of how far you've come.

How have these key lessons impacted your journey? What will you carry forward, and what will you commit to improving as you continue?

Your Self-Promise Declaration

Now it's time to create your self-promise declaration—your personal commitment to the life you want to create. As you move forward, let this declaration guide you and ensure that the promises you make to yourself align with your long-term vision.

Take a few moments to write your self-promise declaration using these prompts:

What's your ultimate vision for your life? Write about the life you want to create, the values that will guide you, and the impact you want to have.

What self-promises will help you achieve that vision? Reflect on how your promises align with your vision. What specific actions will you take to stay committed to those promises?

How will you stay accountable? Consider how you'll hold yourself accountable. Will you share your journey with someone, journal about it, or set regular reflection check-ins?

What will you do when challenges arise? Write about how you'll stay resilient when life doesn't go according to plan. How will you bounce back and keep moving forward?

Chapter Forty-Five

FINAL THOUGHTS

Stay the Course

The self-promises you've made are more than words—they're your declaration that you won't settle for anything less than the life you deserve. And every time you keep a promise, you're building the foundation for that life.

Keep going. Stay true to your promises, and trust that no matter how tough it gets, every step you take brings you closer to the life you've envisioned. You've got this.

As you near the end of this journey, one thing should be clear: the promises you make to yourself are the foundation of your personal growth, resilience, and fulfilment. Each promise is a declaration of your commitment to live a life that reflects your values, goals, and deepest desires. More than just words, your promises shape who you are, what you become, and the legacy you leave behind.

> No one should stand in your way of becoming the person you need to be. Including yourself.

When you first set out on this path, you may not have fully realised the power a single promise holds. You may have seen it as just a goal or a resolution—a way to improve yourself or reach a milestone. But throughout this book, you've seen how promises are so much more than that. They are the bedrock upon which you build your character, create momentum, and live a life filled with purpose and intention.

Your Journey Forward

The road ahead won't always be easy. There will be moments of doubt, setbacks, and uncertainty. But now, you have the tools to navigate those challenges with resilience, adaptability, and a deep sense of self-compassion. You know the journey is just as important as the destination and that every step forward—no matter how small—brings you closer to living a life that is true to your promises.

Remember, making and keeping promises isn't about perfection. Progress is what it's about. It's about showing up for yourself day after day, even when it's difficult. It's about celebrating your wins, learning from your setbacks, and staying committed to your values and goals. You don't have to be perfect to make a difference—you just have to be persistent.

Every promise you keep, no matter how small, contributes to the person you are becoming. With every promise, you're building a foundation of trust in yourself. You're proving, time and time again, that you can achieve what you set out to do. That trust in yourself is what will carry you through life's challenges and give you the confidence to keep moving forward.

The Ripple Effect of Your Promises

As we explored earlier, the promises you make to yourself don't just impact your life—they have a ripple effect on those around you. Your strength, resilience, and commitment to growth inspire others to do the same. Whether you realise it, you are a role model to those who witness your journey. Every time you keep a promise to yourself, you show others what's possible. You create a legacy of strength and perseverance that will continue to inspire long after you've reached your own goals.

Trusting Yourself

Trust is at the centre of this entire journey. The promises you make to yourself are acts of trust—trusting that you can grow, the resilience to overcome challenges, and the power to shape your own life. Trusting yourself is not about having all the answers or being perfect—it's about believing that you have the strength to keep moving forward, even when the path is unclear.

As you continue your journey, remember to trust in your own capabilities. Trust that you are worthy of the life you want to create. Trust that every promise you make and keep is a step toward building that life. And trust that even when you stumble or fall short, you have the power to get back up, learn from the experience, and continue forward.

Make the Promise

You may or may not fully grasp the principles of making a promise yet, but I can tell you from experience—this approach works. At 52 years old, I'm remarried to Mrs Adams the 3rd. We have a wonderful blended family, and we're getting through challenges together. Life is good, and all of this has been achievable by following the blueprint I've shown you in this book.

So here's my last challenge to you: make the promise to live a life that reflects your true values. Commit to showing up for yourself every day, regardless of the circumstances, and embrace your individuality throughout the journey. Make the promise to embrace the journey, to celebrate your progress, and to learn from your setbacks. Make the promise to live with resilience, compassion, and courage.

And most of all, make the promise to never stop believing in your ability to create a life that is meaningful, fulfilling, and true to who you are.

The Power of a Promise

The power of a promise lies in its ability to change your life—and the lives of those around you. This journey through the book is just the beginning. Now it's time to take everything you've learned and apply it to your own life. You have the tools, the mindset, and the strength to make and keep promises that will shape your future.

Remember: the power to change your life isn't something you need to find outside of yourself. It's already within you. It's in the promises you make, the actions you take, and the trust you build with yourself. So go ahead—make the promise, keep it, and watch as your life transforms in ways you never thought possible.

Final Key Takeaways:

The promises you make to yourself are powerful tools for shaping your life and living in alignment with your true values and goals.

Resilience, flexibility, and self-compassion are essential for navigating setbacks and staying committed to your promises, even when the road gets tough.

The ripple effect of your promises extends far beyond your own life, inspiring others and leaving a lasting legacy of strength and commitment.

Trust in yourself is the foundation of personal growth—trust that you are capable, worthy, and able to create the life you desire.

Make the promise and keep it, knowing that every step forward, no matter how small, contributes to the life you're building and the impact you're making.

CHAPTER FORTY-SIX

THE BLUEPRINT

YOUR GOLDEN PATHWAY

Sometimes in life, we don't even know what we want, and that's okay. It can take years to figure ourselves out, to dig through layers of trauma and doubt that have built up. Our fears, our failures, the deeply seated beliefs we hold about not being "enough" can creep back in, paralyse us, and stop us from moving forward. But I'm living proof that when you take care of yourself—physically, mentally, emotionally—everything else falls into place.

> That is why I said at the beginning of the book, there isn't a one quick fix for your life. It is a combination of learning through experience, finding out who you truly are, and then using promises to enhance the areas you are struggling with.

We also all need recognition for what we achieve. Whether it's a pat on the back from ourselves or from someone else, it's a basic human need. It's what gives us the energy to keep going. This blueprint is designed to keep you on that path—leading you to the promises you've made, to the rewards, to the celebrations that ensure you stay motivated and driven.

The secret lies in transforming your promise into your passion. You have to want it so badly that nothing—not doubt, no fear, no setbacks—can take it away from you. You have to live, breathe, and embody that promise every single day.

It's not about occasional bursts of motivation or half-hearted attempts at change. It's about doing the work—consistently, relentlessly, with heart and soul. That's how change happens. You can't master something unless you invest time, effort, and energy into it. The more you practise, the better the results.

So here's the truth: If you stick to this framework, if you follow the blueprint I've laid out, your life will change. I guarantee it. Just give it a go. Give it your all and watch where the magic takes you.

The Power of Your Promise

> The truth of life is this: we cannot control what happens to us. Tomorrow is uncertain, and the events that unfold—good or bad—will shape our lives in ways we can't predict. But here's the unshakable truth: we are in complete control of how we rise. No setback, no heartbreak, no failure can destroy you—unless you allow it.

Every single time life knocked me down—when I lost everything, when I thought it was all over—something better came along. But here's the surprise: it wasn't luck. It wasn't fate. It was my decision to get back up. I refused to stay down. I refused to let life dictate my story. I wanted more, and I made sure I went out and got it.

You have to want it. You have to want it so fiercely, so completely, that nothing can stand in your way. This isn't about hoping. This is about knowing. Knowing that the moment you plant your flag and say, "This is my life, and I will let nothing stop me," everything changes.

Because here's the hard truth: you will achieve nothing unless you want it with every fibre of your being.

This isn't just about setting goals. It's about making a promise. Your promise is the stake in the ground. It's the line you draw in the sand—the declaration that says, "This is who I am. This is what I'm going to achieve, no matter what." Your promise is your passion—it's the fuel that ignites the fire in your soul. When you make that promise, you agree with yourself that nothing will stand in your way.

> Stop waiting for someone to pull you out of bed in the morning. No one is coming to save you. The only person who can change your life is the one staring back at you in the mirror. The day you choose to rise—that's the day your world shifts.

Make Your Promise Your Passion

Yes, you might experience failed marriages. Yes, you might lose jobs, businesses, friends. You might lose everything. But those failures aren't proof that you're broken—they're proof that you had the courage to try. Success doesn't come because you never failed—it comes because you kept going despite those failures. It's because you made a promise to yourself that nothing would stop you.

What will it be? Will you let life drag you down, chew you up, and spit you out? Or will you decide, right now, that enough is enough?

Because the truth is, you are in control of who you become. When you step onto the path as your authentic self—when you walk that path with unwavering belief in your capabilities—nothing can stop you.

The only thing standing between you and the life you deserve is your belief in your own power.

Your purpose on this earth is not to simply exist. Your purpose here is to thrive. To build, to create, to add value to this world in a way that only you can. But you won't do that if you don't step into the arena. If you don't make that promise to yourself and live it every single day, then life will just happen to you.

> Don't let life just happen.
> Make life happen for you.
> You Are the Force of Change

People need your strength. They need to see someone who will keep fighting, even when the road gets tough. They need to see someone who keeps their promises—because every promise you keep inspires others to do the same.

Remember this: people once thought the four-minute mile was impossible. But once someone broke it? Suddenly, everyone believed they could do it, and they did. Life can be whatever you want it to be, but you have to believe in it first. Want it so badly that nothing can stop you.

Your Time is Now

So here's my challenge to you: Make that promise. Make it big. Make it bold and powerful in a way that it will never be broken. Let it be your guiding light, the flame that continues to burn through all of life's challenges.

> This is your moment. Your life. Your promise.

Live your life fully. Live it boldly, with passion and purpose. Be your authentic self. Be kind, be present, and keep showing up every single day. When you make a promise to yourself, and you keep it, you will change everything—not just for you, but for everyone around you.

Now is your time.

Make the promise. Keep it. And watch your life transform in ways you never thought possible.

All my love, Scott

CHAPTER FORTY-SEVEN

AUTHOR BIO: SCOTT ADAMS

Hi, I'm Scott Adams, a resilience coach, father, and self-made author, and I've dedicated my life to helping people find their footing through life's roughest moments. It hasn't been an easy road for me, either. From battling fear, self-doubt, and relentless setbacks, I've spent decades working on my own promises to myself, just as I now encourage others to do. My mission is simple but powerful: to guide people, one promise at a time, toward the lives they were meant to lead.

This book was born out of that mission—and believe me, writing it wasn't without its challenges. I, too, wrestled with procrastination, imposter syndrome, and the fear of exposing my story to the world. But I made a commitment to see it through, inspired by so many of my clients and friends who have shown me just how transformative a single promise can be. One story that has stayed with me is Jo's, a close friend and client who went through a devastating breakup and was facing severe self-doubt and depression. We worked day by day, rebuilding her confidence, piecing together her vision, and crafting promises to help her live for herself. Today, Jo is travelling the world, running marathons, and has found the soulmate she once thought she'd never meet. Her journey lit a fire in me to share my story, to show just how powerful a promise can be.

This book is far from polished—I'm aware of that, and as a self-published author, I'm learning. But I've put it out there because I made a promise: to face my own fears and share my story honestly. Every word in this book is a step in fulfilling that promise, and I hope it serves as a reminder that we don't have to be perfect to make an impact. This is my commitment to you: I'll keep learning, refining, and improving this work, so it can serve those who need it the most.

If this book has struck a chord with you, please consider leaving a review. I value your feedback deeply, and it will help me as I work to make this book—and future ones—even better. I believe we're all on this journey together, learning to build better lives, one promise at a time. Let's create a ripple effect of change by supporting each other and inspiring others to find strength, resilience, and fulfilment through the promises we keep to ourselves.

Thank you for being part of this journey. Let's keep changing lives, one promise at a time. And I hope you will drop in and find me at unlockyo urpromise.com

With gratitude and hope, all my best wishes Scott Adams